Star Light, Star Bright

Whole-Language Activities

with Nursery Rhymes

Beth Rose Neiderman
Jean Naples Kuhn

⩕ Addison-Wesley Publishing Company

Menlo Park, California • Reading, Massachussetts • New York
Don Mills, Ontario • Wokingham, England • Amsterdam • Bonn
Sydney • Singapore • Tokyo • Madrid • San Juan • Paris
Seoul • Milan • Mexico City • Taipei

About the Authors

Beth Rose Neiderman and Jean Naples Kuhn met at the University of Pennsylvania in Philadelphia in 1987. Beth was completing a Bachelor's and Jean a Master's degree in elementary education. Both went on to teach first grade in the Pine Hill School District in New Jersey. There they collaborated on several thematic teaching units, one of which resulted in *Star Light, Star Bright: Whole-Language Activities with Nursery Rhymes*.

Beth returned to Penn and earned a Master's degree in reading, writing, and literacy. She is currently teaching kindergarten in Woodstown, New Jersey. Jean has taught in both private and public school and has done consulting work in elementary science education for the Franklin Institute Science Museum in Philadelphia. At this time she is devoting her energies to her two young sons.

Acknowledgments

We wish to thank Drs. Cynthia Paris, James Larkin, Marilyn Cochran-Smith, Ryda Rose, and Morton Botel of the University of Pennsylvania for the untiring efforts and energy they put into educating us.

Additional gratitude is due Drs. Larkin and Paris for reading and commenting on our introduction.

This book is published by Addison-Wesley's Alternative Publishing Group.

Managing Editor: Diane G. Silver
Senior Editor: Lois Fowkes
Production Manager: Janet Yearian
Production Coordinator: Karen Edmonds
Design Manager: Jeff Kelly
Text and Cover Design: Paula Shuhert

Contents

Index of Skills

Introduction

Two children closely examine the candles they dangle from their hands. "It took eight dips to get it this fat—and look, it's still puny!" exclaims one. "Yeah," agrees the other, "the chandler had a hard job in the old days." The two are waiting for the wax on their hand-dipped candles to cool before dipping again. On this afternoon, the first grade classes have taken over the entire gym. While one group makes candles, another is involved in the Jack Be Nimble jumping contest. The rest are gathered around a chalkboard recording the jumping results on their bar graphs. All the children are intent on their tasks. The room is filled with the buzz of conversation, punctuated with frequent cheers from the jumpers.

This afternoon is not a special treat given to the students because they've finished their classwork—it *is* their classwork. They are studying a thematic unit on nursery rhymes, and by now they know that in thematic units one thing always leads to another. This particular unit started with reading "Jack Be Nimble," then doing activities with rhymes. Next were discussions and research into candles and fire. One rainy morning the lights were turned off and the class observed two candles burning: one in a big jar, one in a small jar. All along, students have been keeping track of their thoughts in journals. They've also written some class books and shared them with people in the school. Because of their experiences, words like *oxygen, observation, chandler,* and *superstition* have crept into their vocabularies and are now there to stay.

This is experience-based learning. Here the children learn by doing. They measure how far they jump in the Jack Be Nimble jumping contest. They make a graph to tell a picture story of the class's results. They sample craftsmanship firsthand by making candles.

The discussions, reading, and writing that result from this study are in depth and meaningful. The children are truly interested and invested in their learning, and it shows.

Why Thematic Teaching?

This book is a thematic program that reunites separate parts of the curriculum under subthemes drawn from the nursery rhymes: "Jack Be Nimble"—candles, fire; "Star Light, Star Bright"—astronomy, space travel; "One, Two, Buckle My Shoe"—counting; "Jack and Jill"—water. We developed the program to provide a broad context in which our students could explore language. We built it based on our students' interests, then followed their leads in exploration.

Engaging students in purposeful activities drawn from a common theme is not a new idea. One hundred years ago, educator and philosopher John Dewey used this approach to teaching at the Dewey School of the University of Chicago. Dewey believed that children learned by confronting problems they encountered while doing activities that were interesting to them. He recognized the value of the real-life experiences that children brought with them to school. These experiences allowed the teachers to draw references for the children, and so to go from the known to the unknown.

Every teacher needs to cover certain subjects in the course of the school year. Dewey's philosophy was to integrate course material in the same way that people naturally strive to integrate the knowledge they acquire. His idea of integrated teaching—seen here as thematic units—is alive and well today in many public and private schools. The themes of these units are so complex and vast that they offer inexhaustible possibilities for study. Most importantly, they are real. Students are genuinely interested in learning about the topics and consequently invest impressive amounts of time and energy into their study.

Thematic units offer a child-centered approach to teaching. They give students choices of authentic, relevant activities, and allow students a say in the organization and planning of the unit. (Goodman, 1986) Because the students have a voice in the planning, they feel that the work is their own—not just schoolwork imposed upon them.

Many of the "Facts and Ideas for Discussion" and activities in this unit deal with topics not ordinarily discussed in most first-grade classes. For example, the "Star Light, Star Bright" chapter includes an activity that explores astronomy. The children hear and discuss stories about Orion and Andromeda, then make "Star Gazers" from aluminum foil and paper towel rolls.

Each child takes something different from these activities. Some may remember the stories, others the constellation configurations. There may be no one who appreciates just how ancient these stories are. We teach with Vygotsky's "zone of proximal development" always in mind. Vygotsky based his idea on the fact that learning doesn't happen in neat, predictable units. In mathematics, for example, the teachers may observe a student who manipulates beads to find the answer to 2 + 3. One day the student may volunteer the answer without using the beads, only to go back to them for the same problem the next day. This back-and-forth movement between the concrete and abstract stages of development represents Vygotsky's zone. The way we teach for the zone is to provide a range of challenges for the class so that each child may advance at his or her own rate. (Vygotsky, 1978)

Thematic units attend to the skills and objectives that the teacher feels are necessary to language and literacy development in her or his students. They are based on the belief that children have an innate curiosity and strive to develop language, not for its own sake but as a way to learn and communicate ideas about their worlds. (Strickland, 1989)

Why Whole Language?

Language is composed of four interdependent subsystems: (1) phonological (for oral language) and graphic/graphophonic (for written language); (2) syntactic; (3) semantic; and (4) pragmatic. Traditionally, these subsystems have been split and studied separately. The theory was that once a child understood the parts, she or he could properly use language. Edelsky argues that when language is broken into these parts it ceases to have meaning and consequently ceases to be language. (Edelsky, 1991)

Most children accept the need for reading exercises, much as they would accept doing drills for a sport. It is when the exercises replace the actual reading that they often become discouraged. (Bettelheim and Zelan, 1982) Continuing the sports analogy, dribbling a ball up and down a court may help the eye-hand coordination necessary in basketball, but the sport itself demands many more skills used simultaneously. It is the game itself that is exhilarating and satisfying, as well as being the best context for learning from both successes and failures.

Ken Goodman tells us that language learning is easy when it is authentic and relevant. Children are driven by a need to communicate. By getting the entire class involved in cooperative activities, uncountable interactions occur in which the students observe, describe, and question. What is more, the group's shared experiences give them something in common, while adding to their background knowledge. (Goodman, 1986)

Lytle and Botel support the idea that letters and sounds have no meaning apart from text. They recommend using poems and folk rhymes to investigate language. They suggest that from these texts, "teachers can choose sound/spelling patterns to emphasize (i.e., can help students notice) what words with similar sounds have in common. These activities integrate decoding and encoding within meaningful language experiences, thus diminishing the need for covering separately each of the so-called subjects of phonics, spelling, grammar, etc." (Lytle and Botel, 1988)

The activities suggested for the Basic Format give students opportunities to investigate language closely. Included are oral chanting, sentence and word matching, oral and written cloze, and word-making activities. During the unit the children spend a lot of time with the rhymes. You'll hear them chanting them as they wait in the lunch line or run around the playground. They get to know them so well that they feel they "own" them. Consequently, the rhymes and the words in them serve as strong reference points. In writing, for example, when a child asks how to spell *right,* a teacher points out the similarities the word has to many of the rhyming words in "Star Light, Star Bright." Because of the association, the child realizes that this word is not entirely new.

The whole-language teacher respects the students' role in their own learning. She or he follows the students' leads, acting as coach or facilitator, rather than as drill master in learning. (*Note:* While using the unit, if you notice that your students are more interested in one part than another, make the most of that section. Spend extra time with it—develop more activities on your own. We give an example of a day's format but caution that it is only a *suggestion.* Practice Yetta Goodman's "kid-watching." Trust and follow the lead of your students. Forcing every activity on every child, disregarding individual interests, makes a basal out of the unit and is not its intended use.)

Why Nursery Rhymes?

Nursery rhymes offer language patterns and vocabulary not found in most primers. In addition, they are rich in context. Each reflects an entire thought—tells a miniature story that stands alone. This is advantageous to beginning readers who learn to refer to the context in order to make attempts at words they don't know. They practice metacognition, continually asking themselves, "Does this make sense?" Metacognition is a skill accomplished readers take for granted, and one that beginning readers need in order to succeed.

Although it is not necessarily true that most children have had prior exposure to the rhymes, many have. For those who haven't, these rhymes are interesting and easy to learn. Also, children self-select the rhymes and enjoy sharing them with one another.

The activities found in this unit might be categorized "enrichment" in traditional reading books, most often with only the advanced readers getting to do them. We used the activities with the whole class, and they led to lively discourse, detailed journal entries, shared reading, and more. The rhymes served as jumping-off points for inquiries into other subjects. For example, during our study of "Star Light, Star Bright," the children enthusiastically shared stories of occasions when they had observed stars. Some knew what the Big Dipper looked like and were interested to know that it was just one of many constellations. Soon we were off to the library for more information about stars and constellation stories. That was when the "Star Gazers" and "Connect the Stars" activities joined the unit.

Nursery rhymes allow students a view of the big picture, expose them to the rhythm and rhyme in language, and to a writer's entire thought. When students have a whole work under their belts—*and when they display a need for direct instruction*—then is the time for close examination of the subsystems of language. But by experiencing the rhyme first, they are doing what teachers hope their students will do—they are reading.

References

Bettelheim, B., and K. Zelan. *On Learning to Read*. New York: Random House, 1982.

Dewey, J. *Democracy and Education*. New York: Macmillan Publishing Co., 1916.

Edelsky, D., B. Altwerger, and B. Flores. *Whole Language: What's the Difference?* Portsmouth: Heinemann, 1991.

Goodman, K. *What's Whole in Whole Language?* Portsmouth: Heinemann, 1986.

Goodman, Y. "Kidwatching: Evaluating Written Language Development." *Australian Journal of Reading,* Vol. 5, No. 3, pp. 120–128, August 1982.

Lytle, S., and M. Botel. *The Pennsylvania Framework: Reading, Writing, and Talking Across the Curriculum*. Harrisburg: Pennsylvania Department of Education, 1988.

Smith, Frank. *Reading Without Nonsense*. New York: Teacher's College Press, 1985.

Strickland, D.S., and L. M. Morrow. *Emerging Literacy: Young Children Learn to Read and Write*. Newark: International Reading Association, 1989.

Vygotsky, L. *Mind In Society*. Cambridge: Harvard University Press, 1978.

Sharing Nursery Rhymes with the Class: A Basic Format

The following five-day basic format is a suggested model for use when introducing nursery rhymes to the class. It is based on concepts developed by Drs. Morton Botel and Jo Ann Seaver in *Language Arts Phonics*. It is by no means the only appropriate process for language study. Teachers may find that they need to spend more time on some activities and less time on others. This day-to-day format is only suggested; teachers are encouraged to adapt this model to meet the needs of their students.

The activities described in subsequent chapters can be used to enhance learning of the nursery rhymes. These hands-on experiences integrate other areas of the curriculum such as science, math, social studies, art, drama, and music. During these activities, students are encouraged to write, read, talk, and listen for a variety of meaningful purposes. Again, these activities are only suggestions. Teachers should make choices based on the students' interests.

Day 1: Introducing the Rhyme

Discussion: Day 1 activities focus on the enjoyment of the entire poem. As children chant the rhyme, they quickly learn the words and get a feel for the rhythm. The poem should be made a part of the classroom so that children can go back to it and reread it at their own pace.

Materials: chart paper
marker
composition book or homemade book
Nursery Rhyme blackline master (1 copy for each student)

(A) Write the rhyme on chart paper and read it to the class. Point to the words as you read them and invite the students to join in. As students hear each word and see it pointed out, they begin to develop basic sight word vocabulary as well as form letter/sound relationships.

Echo-read the poem by reading a line, then having the class repeat it. This can be varied by having a student or group of students read a line while the rest of the class repeats it.

Once the class is familiar with the rhyme, practice chanting it together. Students can clap their hands or play simple instruments such as triangles, tambourines, or bells to experience the beat and rhythm of the poem.

(B) Have the students examine word detail by picking out any rhyming words they hear. How do the words look the same? Which letters are the same? Which are different? Use the marker to highlight rhyming words or letters.

(C) Make poetry books by having each child glue a copy of the rhyme into a composition or homemade book. (Each time a new rhyme is learned, have children add it to their books. At the end of the nursery rhyme unit, the children will have a book of poems that they can read by themselves. As poetry is introduced in other units, students can add the new poems to their books.)

Children can practice reading the new poem to a partner. This gives every student a chance to practice reading the poem aloud. Partners should be instructed to help each other decode unknown words. Partners can also practice echo reading and chanting the poem together. Later, the books can be sent home so that the children can practice reading them to an adult or older sibling.

Day 2: Sentence Matching

Discussion: Chanting and group work provide a safe environment for beginning readers. Children will eventually feel secure enough to take risks, which in turn will help them develop good learning habits. Group work provides shared experiences for children who come from diverse backgrounds.

Materials: rhyme on chart paper from Day 1
sentence strips
colored markers
self-adhesive magnets (if blackboard is magnetic) or pocket chart (if blackboard is not magnetic)

(A) Have the group chant the poem written on the chart paper. Point to the words in print as the children read. Have a group of students act out the poem as the rest of the class reads it.

(B) Use a different color marker to write each line of the rhyme on a sentence strip. Have the children match the strips to the lines in the printed rhyme. The children can then try putting the strips in the correct order. If you have a magnetic blackboard, attach small magnets to the back of the strips for display on the board. A pocket chart will work too. Children could also hold the strips and rearrange themselves in the right order.

Day 3: Word Matching/Syntax/Oral Cloze

Discussion: The matching and syntax activities that follow allow children to examine word parts in the context of the whole poem.

Materials: rhyme on chart paper from Day 1
words to nursery rhyme written on 3-by-5-inch cards

(A) As the children become comfortable with the sentence strips, they can begin to investigate each word more closely. Using the 3-by-5-inch word cards, match each card to the words on the chart, discussing letter positions and sounds. You may want to pass out the cards to the children and have them try to match the card to the word on the chart.

Chant the poem again, having each child hold up his or her card as it is read. Have students come to the chart to confirm their choices. As they become familiar with the words, they are adding to their basic sight word vocabulary.

(B) When the children are ready, try an oral cloze activity. Read the rhyme to the children, leaving out some words. When you pause, have the children say the missing word as you point to it on the chart. For example, you read "Jack be _____"; the children say the word "nimble" as you point to it on the chart.

Day 4: Written Cloze with the Class

Discussion: With the words and meter of the rhyme now firmly in their minds, students have a solid basis for determining which words are missing in the written cloze activity. If they are unsure of spelling, they refer to the chart paper for verification.

Materials: rhyme on chart paper from Day 1
self-stick removable notes
Cloze Activity blackline master (1 for each student)

(A) Review the word cards. Prepare the class for a written cloze activity by doing visual cloze as a group: Place self-stick removable notes over a word in each line of the rhyme. Have the children predict which word is missing as you read the rhyme. Uncover the words to confirm their predictions.

(B) After the whole group has practiced thoroughly, have the children work with partners to complete the cloze activity. The partner work is important here because as the children work together, they are sharing ideas and practicing oral language as they explain and defend their choices. The children compare the incomplete rhyme to the completed version, referring to the latter to fill in the blanks. A great deal of reading takes place as the partners read both versions to determine whether they are correct.

Day 5: Written Cloze/Visual Context Clues/Word Matching

Discussion: The word-making activity allows children to examine letter patterns that they have experienced through the nursery rhyme. Understanding of these patterns may transfer to their own reading and writing.

Materials: Cloze Activity blackline master (1 for each student)
poetry books from Day 1
Word-Making blackline masters (1 for each student)
lined paper (1 sheet for every 2 students)
an enlarged version of the Word-Making blackline master, or a copy of the Word-Making blackline master on a transparency
scissors

(A) As a review, have the students complete the written Cloze Activity blackline master on their own. These can be corrected as a class, or exchanged and checked by partners.

(B) For the word-making activity, have students cut their copies of the blackline masters into individual cards. Using the enlarged cards or the transparency, show children how to make words by combining the initial consonant with the word ending (for example, $k + ick = kick$). Individual children can demonstrate word making by holding enlarged cards and rearranging themselves to make words, or by manipulating the transparency cards on the overhead projector. Words created can be written on the board.

With partners, students can use their own cards to create words. Partners can write down the words they made on the lined paper. These words can be compiled into personal word pattern dictionaries (students write the pattern—such as *ick*—at the top of the page, then list and illustrate the words they have created for this pattern). These pages can be stored in folders, then stapled together to make a book at the end of the unit, or written on pages in a composition or home-made book. Pattern dictionaries can also be made into class Big Books for future reference.)

(C) Have children brainstorm different images the rhyme brings to mind. Have children put examples of illustrations on the board. Allow time for the students to provide their own visual context clues for the rhyme by illustrating it in their poetry books.

(D) Reproduce the "Book To Illustrate" blackline masters for "Jack and Jill" and "One, Two, Buckle My Shoe." Show the students how to construct the books (see Overviews of Blackline Masters for those chapters), then read the texts together.

Have the children draw pictures to go with the text. Illustrating requires that the children read and understand the text; subsequently their own pictures serve as context clues when they reread the rhyme.

(E) Reproduce the Handwriting blackline master for children to complete and trace as seatwork or homework.

Chapter One

Jack Be Nimble

Jack be nimble,
Jack be quick,
Jack jump over
The candlestick!

Jack Be Nimble Curriculum Web

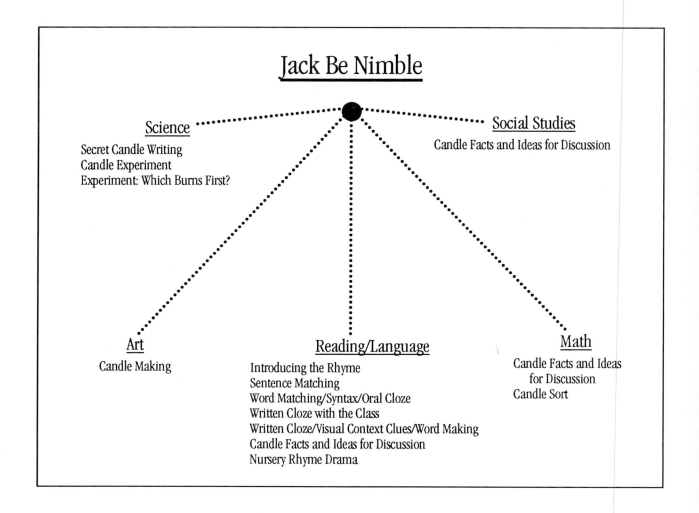

Jack Be Nimble

Science
Secret Candle Writing
Candle Experiment
Experiment: Which Burns First?

Social Studies
Candle Facts and Ideas for Discussion

Art
Candle Making

Reading/Language
Introducing the Rhyme
Sentence Matching
Word Matching/Syntax/Oral Cloze
Written Cloze with the Class
Written Cloze/Visual Context Clues/Word Making
Candle Facts and Ideas for Discussion
Nursery Rhyme Drama

Math
Candle Facts and Ideas
for Discussion
Candle Sort

Related Literature

Fire! Fire! Said Mrs. McGuire, by Bill Martin, Jr. (Holt, Rinehart, and Winston, 1970)

Firefighters, by Robert Mass (Scholastic, 1991)

Little Nancy Etticoat (Nursery Rhyme)

Night Fire!, by Mary Jesse Parker (Scholastic, 1991)

Candle Facts and Ideas for Discussion

1. Candles are usually made using one of three methods:
   a. Dipping: Wicks are cut and weights are put at the end of them to keep them straight. The wicks are then dipped into melted wax. A candle that is 3/4 inch in diameter must be dipped 24 to 30 times. This used to be done by hand; now it is usually done by machines.
   b. Rolling: Wax is kneaded and rolled onto a sheet, then wound around a wick until it is the right size.
   c. Molding: Wicks are placed into molds. Wax is poured into the molds and let set until hard.

2. We blow out candles on a birthday cake because people used to believe that by blowing out the candles they were blowing away the bad luck of past years. That is why we put a candle for each year of age on our birthday cakes.

3. In England, people used to jump over candles to tell their fortunes. Jumping over the candle without putting out the flame assured the jumper a full year of good luck. That is probably why Jack jumped over the candlestick.

   Have the children try their luck at jumping over a (unlighted) candlestick. See the Overview of Blackline Masters on page 11 for a description of an activity that features jumping, measuring, and graphing.

4. This might be a good time to discuss fire safety, pointing out the dangers of jumping over a lighted candle.

5. *Nimble* means "quick" or "capable." You may want to have the class try to guess the meaning from the context of the rhyme.

6. Candles are used for a variety of purposes. Together with the class, brainstorm different types of candles and what they are used for. These can be listed on chart paper or on the board.

7. There are specific names for different craftspeople. A chandler is a candle maker. A cooper is a barrel maker and a smith is someone who makes or repairs metal objects. In the past, these names sometimes became the last names of the craftspeople. If you know someone whose last name is Cooper, Smith, or Chandler, he or she may be descended from a craftsperson. Ask students whether they know any other last names that might have come from someone's craft.

Nursery Rhyme Drama

Drama is an effective and enjoyable way to develop comprehension, oral vocabulary, and even basic sight word vocabulary. Here are a few suggestions for using drama with "Jack Be Nimble."

Procedure

1. Have students pretend to be:
   a melting candle
   lighting a candle
   walking with a lighted candle
   blowing out birthday candles

2. Together with the class, brainstorm words for other ways Jack could have gotten over the candlestick (*walk, run, leap,* and so on). List these on the board or on chart paper. You may want to introduce some words that the children don't already know (e.g., *amble, strut, saunter*).

   Read the poem substituting one of the brainstormed words for *jump,* and have the children act it out. For example:

   Jack be nimble,
   Jack be quick,
   Jack *stroll* over
   The candlestick!

3. Write a different verb on each of several 3-by-5-inch cards. Give each card to a student or a small group of students (when handing out a card, whisper the word on it to the student or group so that they know what it says). The student or group acts out the poem using the verb on the card. The rest of the class tries to guess what word is on the card.

Candle Making

Materials

- 10 lbs wax (available at craft stores)

- wax dye (if desired)

- wick (allow 6 inches for each candle)

- 2 one-pound coffee cans

- a two-burner stove

- 2 saucepans

- water

- metal washers (1 for each wick)

- 8-by-10-inch scraps of paper to catch drips and act as name labels

- a knife or screwdriver (for adult use only)

- pot holders or mitts

Children learn by doing. Dipping their own candles gives students a glimpse of how things were done before modern technology. This shared activity opens opportunities for discussion, experiential writing, and fun.

Note: This activity requires 2 or 3 adults.

Procedure

Prepare wicks ahead of time by cutting them into 6-inch lengths and tying a washer to one end of each piece (the washer serves as a weight to hold the wick straight). Use the knife or screwdriver to break the wax into small chunks. It melts faster this way.

Have an adult heat the water in the saucepans on the stove to a slow simmer. Put the coffee cans in the saucepans and add the wax, a few pieces at a time. The wax level must be high enough so that you can dip without bending the wick (be careful, the coffee cans get hot!). If dye is used, add it according to the instructions on the packet.

Regulate the water temperature as the children begin dipping their candles. If the wax is too hot, it will melt what has already accumulated on the wick. If it is too cold, the candles will begin to look bumpy or uneven.

Have each child use a piece of paper with her or his name on it to catch the drips. After children dip their candles, they go to the end of the line to wait for another turn. Lines of at least 10-15 students work well because this allows time for the wax to dry and harden between dippings. The number of dips will determine how thick the candles are. Time is your main limit because it dictates how many turns each child gets.

Candle Making (continued)

When the children have finished dipping their candles, have them hold them for another minute or so to let the wax cool. Then they can set the candles on their own pieces of paper to let them cool completely.

Extension 1: Later that day or the next day, have the children explain to a class visitor (school secretary, principal, teacher) how they made their candles. This is an oral language as well as a sequencing activity.

Extension 2: Make a "How To Make Candles" book or poster by sequencing each step. These can be illustrated with photos taken during the activity or with student drawings.

Secret Candle Writing

Materials

- white construction paper (1 sheet for each student)

- white candles (small groups can share these)

- iodine

- water

- newspaper

- paper towels

Paper contains starch. Iodine, which is usually brown, becomes blue or purple when it comes into contact with starch. When iodine touches white paper, it turns the paper blue.

Note: Iodine is poisonous if swallowed. It should be handled only by the teacher.

Procedure

Have the children put their names on one side of the paper. On the other side, tell them to write a message using the white candle (press hard!). The message will not be visible at this point.

Mix about 15 drops of iodine with a cup of water (add enough iodine so that the mixture looks like tea).

Put children's message papers on some newspaper. Rub a paper towel soaked in the iodine/water mixture over each message paper. The message should remain white, while the rest of the paper turns blue. This happens because the wax from the candle protects the paper from the iodine. The secret message can now be read!

Extension: While the iodine is out, you might want to try testing different foods for starch. Have the students observe as you place a drop of iodine on pieces of different fruits, a piece of potato, a piece of bread, or whatever foods you wish. If starch is present, a drop of iodine will turn the food blue or purple. Record results on a picture graph.

Candle Sort

Materials

■ A wide variety of new and/or used candles—purchased at a thrift shop, yard sale, or flea market or brought from home by the children

This activity gives students practice sorting and classifying in a variety of ways.

Procedure

Divide the class into small groups.

Give each group 10 to 15 candles and have them sort them in whatever way they choose.

Have each group explain the way they chose to sort their candles. Did they sort by size? Color? Shape? Use? Is there another way they could sort the same group of candles?

Extension: Have each group make a pattern with their candles (for example, red, blue, red, blue; thin, fat, thin, fat; upside down, right side up, etc.). Discuss the different pattern each group made. Groups can record their patterns onto paper. This activity could also be set up in a learning center.

Candle Experiment

Materials

- 4 candles (2 of the same size, 2 of different sizes)

- 3 wide-mouth jars (2 of the same size, 1 much larger)

- modeling clay

- matches

- pot holders

Fire needs oxygen to burn. This fact can be demonstrated using the simple experiments outlined below. For these experiments, allow the students to ask questions and make observations after each procedure. Use the board to record students' observations and predictions. Later, these can be recorded onto a chart.

Procedure

Put modeling clay in the bottom of one of the jars and set a candle in it. Light the candle and let it burn for about 15 seconds. Using a pot holder (the jar might get hot), put the lid on the jar and close it so that no air gets in. Record the students' observations.

Variation 1: Use two jars of the same size with the same size candles. Follow the procedure above, but leave one jar open. Record students' observations.

Variation 2: Use two jars of the same size with different size candles. Again put the lid on one jar and leave the other one open. Record students' observations.

Variation 3: Use two jars of different sizes with the same size candles. Again put the lid on one jar and leave the other one open. Record students' observations.

Experiment:
Which Burns First?

Materials

- 5 candles of different sizes

- modeling clay

- matches

- 5 paint cups (or similar containers)

Given different-sized candles, which candle will burn for the longest time? The shortest time?

Procedure

Show children the different candles. Ask them to predict which candle will take the longest time to burn. Which will burn in the shortest time? Record students' predictions.

Using modeling clay, set a candle in each paint cup. Put the cups in a safe but visible place, and light the candles.

Compare the predictions with the results and record.

Variation 1: Light three candles that are the same length but have different diameters. At staggered intervals, blow out the candles and have the children measure them. Which are the tallest? How does their height relate to their diameter?

Variation 2: Record what time the experiment starts. Have the students predict what time the candles will go out. Record the time each candle goes out. How do students' predictions compare to the actual times?

Overview of Blackline Masters

Nursery Rhyme: Jack Be Nimble: See Day 1 of "Sharing Rhymes with the Class: A Basic Format," page x.

Cloze Activity: Partners take turns reading the rhymes, and then determine which words complete the rhyme.

Word Making:– *ick* Words: Children cut out the letters and put them together to make words that end in *ick*. There are two blackline masters of different difficulty levels: one with single letter beginnings, and one with blends and digraphs.

Jumping Contest Certificate and Jumping Bar Graph: The children take turns jumping over a paper candlestick placed on the floor. The candle is made by wrapping, then taping construction paper around an empty food canister similar to those used to hold potato chips or oatmeal. The "flame" is a three-inch piece of fluffy yellow yarn, pulled through a hole that has been punched in the center of the lid.

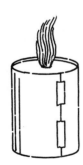

The distance is measured from the starting line of a child's jump to the spot where her or his feet come down on the floor. The length of the jump is recorded on the Jumping Contest Certificates.

After everyone has jumped, the teacher lists on the board all the lengths jumped. The children record the class results on the Jumping Bar Graph by coloring in one box for each person who has jumped a certain length.

Handwriting: Children fill in their own names in place of *Jack,* then trace the rhyme as a handwriting exercise. This can be done for seatwork or for homework.

Jack Be Nimble

Jack be nimble,

Jack be quick,

Jack jump over

The candlestick!

Jack Be Nimble

Jack be nimble,

Jack be quick,

Jack jump over

The candlestick!

Jack Be Nimble

Jack be nimble,

Jack be quick,

Jack jump over

The candlestick!

Jack Be Nimble

Jack be nimble,

Jack be quick,

Jack jump over

The candlestick!

Name ————————————————————

Partner's Name ——————————————

Jack be nimble,
Jack be quick,
Jack jump over
The candlestick!

Fill in the blanks:

Jack _____ nimble,

Jack be _____,

_____ jump over

The candlestick!

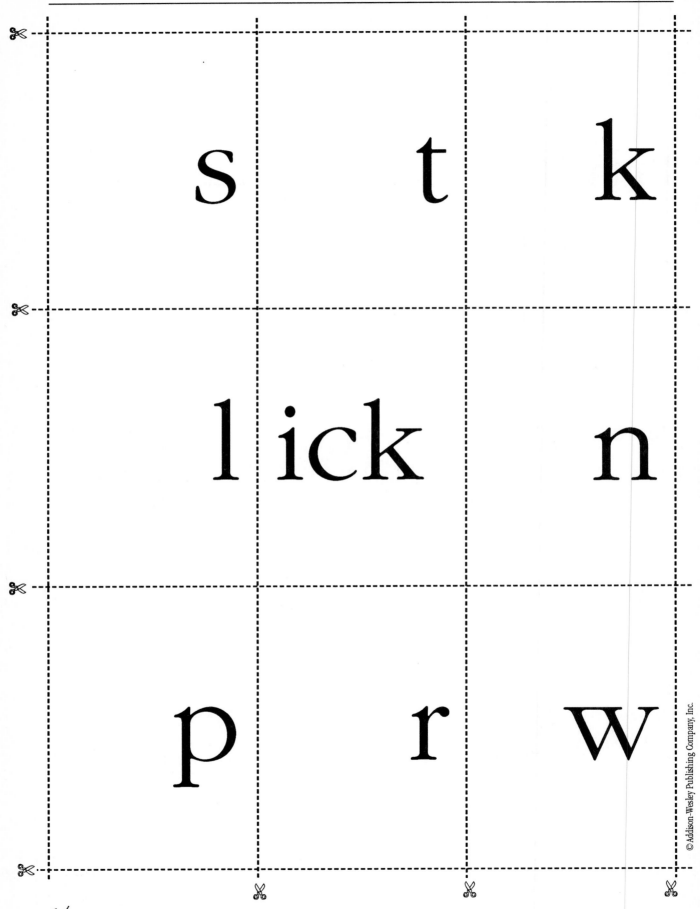

s   t   k

l ick   n

p   r   w

Word Making: *-ick* Words 1

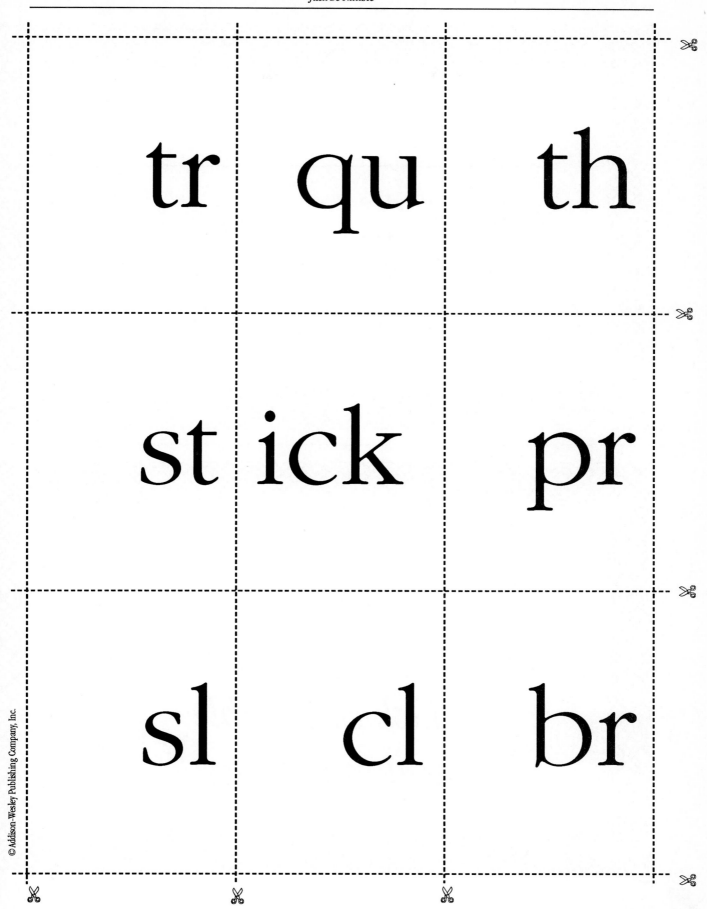

tr | qu | th

st | ick | pr

sl | cl | br

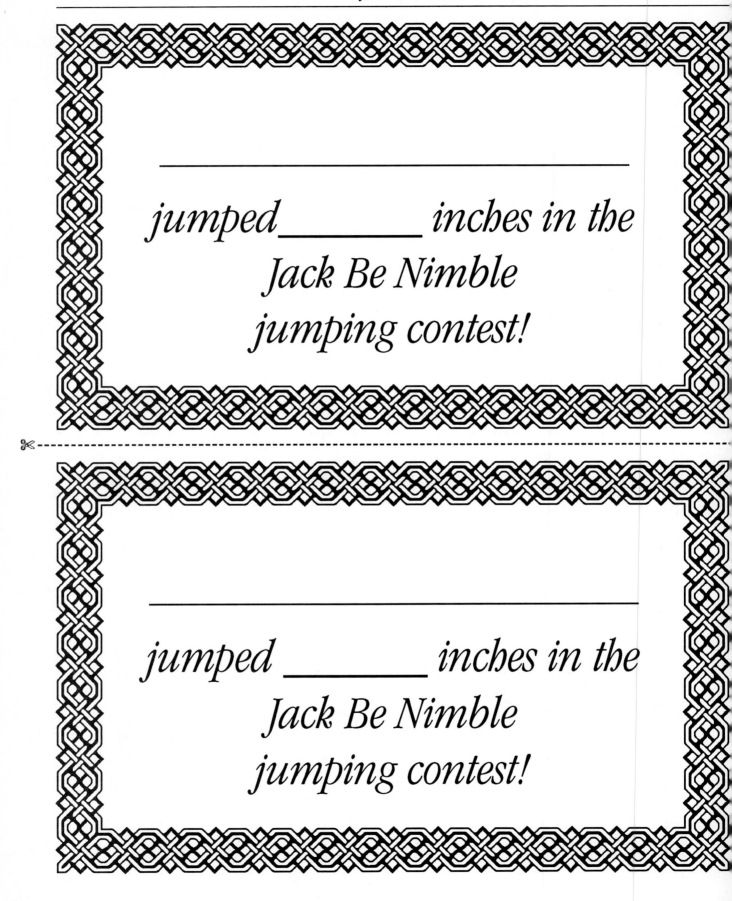

_____

jumped_____ inches in the
Jack Be Nimble
jumping contest!

_____

jumped _____ inches in the
Jack Be Nimble
jumping contest!

Name————————

Show how far people in your group jumped.

Number of people who jumped

	2 Feet	2 1/2 Feet	3 Feet	3 1/2 Feet	4 Feet	4 1/2 Feet	5 Feet	5 1/2 Feet	6 Feet	6 1/2 Feet
20										
19										
18										
17										
16										
15										
14										
13										
12										
11										
10										
9										
8										
7										
6										
5										
4										
3										
2										
1										
0										

Distance Jumped

Jumping Bar Graph

Name _____

Write your name in the blanks and trace the rhyme.

_____ be nimble,

_____ be quick,

_____ jump over

The candlestick!

Chapter Two

Star Light, Star Bright

Star light, star bright,
First star I see tonight—
I wish I may,
I wish I might
Have the wish
I wish tonight.

Star Light, Star Bright
Curriculum Web

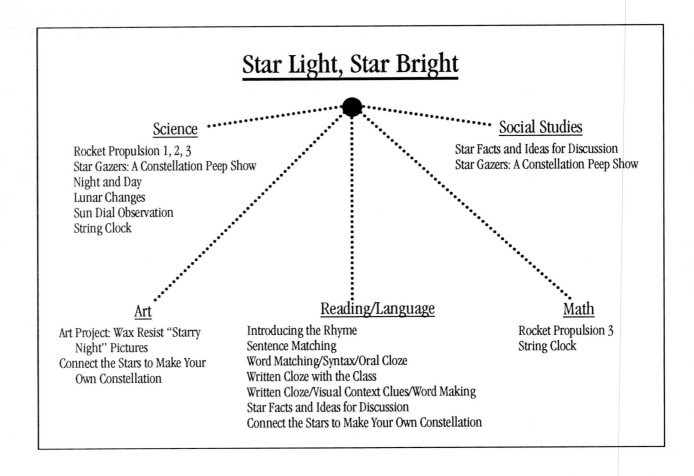

Star Light, Star Bright

Science
Rocket Propulsion 1, 2, 3
Star Gazers: A Constellation Peep Show
Night and Day
Lunar Changes
Sun Dial Observation
String Clock

Social Studies
Star Facts and Ideas for Discussion
Star Gazers: A Constellation Peep Show

Art
Art Project: Wax Resist "Starry
  Night" Pictures
Connect the Stars to Make Your
  Own Constellation

Reading/Language
Introducing the Rhyme
Sentence Matching
Word Matching/Syntax/Oral Cloze
Written Cloze with the Class
Written Cloze/Visual Context Clues/Word Making
Star Facts and Ideas for Discussion
Connect the Stars to Make Your Own Constellation

Math
Rocket Propulsion 3
String Clock

Related Literature

A Day In Space, by Suzanne Lord and Jolie Epstein (Scholastic, 1986)

Follow the Drinking Gourd, by Jeannette Winter (Alfred A. Knopf, 1988)

Glow In the Dark Constellations, by C.E. Thompson (Grosset and Dunlap, 1989)

The Magic Schoolbus Lost In the Solar System, by Joanna Cole (Scholastic, 1990)

Many Moons, by James Thurber (Scholastic, 1943)

Space Songs, by Myra Cohn Livingston (Holiday House, 1988)

Van Gogh, by Mike Venezia (Children's Press, 1988)

Star Facts and Ideas for Discussion

1. The sun is a very small star. It appears much bigger than other stars, however, because it is the closest star to the earth. This idea can be demonstrated to the children by having a tall child and a small child stand side by side on the playground. Ask the taller child to move slowly away from the group. As the child gets farther away, he or she will look smaller. You might also want to point out how small other objects (such as trees or airplanes) look when they are far away.

2. Although the stars are always shining, we can't see them during the day because the sun is too bright. Explain this to the children by shining a flashlight in a well-lit classroom. The flashlight beam is hard to see. Then darken the room as much as possible and shine the flashlight. Now the beam seems very bright.

3. Although the sun appears to rise and set every day, it is actually the earth's movement that creates the illusion of solar motion. As the earth revolves around the sun, it is rotating, or spinning. It takes a year for the earth to revolve around the sun, and a day for the earth to make one complete rotation.

   Dramatize the movements of the earth by having one student portray the stationary sun while another student, acting as the earth, rotates and revolves around the sun.

4. Walking at a steady pace, it would take approximately three years to walk around the earth one time. Walking at the same pace, it would take about 300 years to walk around the sun.

5. Have children brainstorm a list of sounds they hear at night when they go out to observe the stars and the moon. Put a tape recorder outside at night to make a "Night Sounds" tape. Listen to the tape in class and list the sounds the children can identify (for example, crickets, dogs barking, cars).

6. Sing the song, "When You Wish Upon A Star" (write the song on chart paper so that children can follow the words as they sing). Have the children tell, write, or draw the things they would wish for. Ask them whether the teacher or their parents would wish for the same or for different things. Follow the activity with the "I Wish" worksheet.

7. Using sun print paper, take "sun pictures" of objects chosen by the children. (Sun print paper is available in most teacher supply stores, hobby shops, or science stores.)

8. This nursery rhyme talks about wishing on a star. Have children brainstorm a list of other things to wish on (e.g., birthday candles).

9. Share the picture "A Starry Night" by Vincent Van Gogh. The book, *Van Gogh,* by Mike Venezia (Children's Press, Chicago, 1988), provides a copy of this masterpiece along with information on Van Gogh's life and work. The sharing of the picture can be followed by the starry night art project described in this chapter.

Art Project:
Wax Resist "Starry Night" Pictures

Materials

■ white construction paper (1 sheet for each child)

■ crayons

■ black or dark blue watercolor paints

■ paint brushes (the fat kind with lots of bristles works best)

Why doesn't the paint stay on top of the crayon in this activity? The fiber in the paper absorbs the watercolor, while wax resists it. Since crayons are made of wax, everywhere the children color is protected from the watercolors. Places where the children do not color, or color too lightly, are unprotected and so are able to hold the paint.

Procedure

Have the students use their crayons to draw a nighttime scene on the construction paper. Instruct them to press down very hard with their crayons when coloring. The students should include night things such as the moon or stars in their drawings, but should not color in the sky. Explain that they will do this later with their paints.

When the pictures are completed, pass out the watercolors. Tell the children to use wide, sweeping motions to cover the *whole* picture with the black or dark blue paint. (Some children will want to paint only the parts of the paper that are still white. Explain that for this activity they need to paint over what they have drawn as well.) For the best results, the children should paint in one direction.

Have the students predict what will happen when they paint over their picture. These predictions can be told to a partner, written on the board, or recorded in personal journals. After the painting is done, students can comment (orally or in writing) on what happened.

Rocket Propulsion, Part 1

Materials

■ balloons

In this activity, students observe balloons in motion and infer reasons for their motion.

Procedure

Blow up some balloons and have student volunteers hold them so that no air escapes.

Ask for observations of the balloons and record them on the board. Tell the volunteers to let go of the balloons, and then record new observations of the balloons.

Ask the children if they know what caused the balloons to move. The children should infer that the air coming out of the balloons caused them to fly around.

Teacher's Note: Newton's Law: For every action there is an equal and opposite reaction.

Rocket Propulsion, Part 2

Materials

- balloons

- string

- straws

- tape

- plastic bag twist ties

In the previous experiment, the balloons flew all over the room. Rockets and planes are able to fly in one direction because they have fins, wings, and rudders to help steer them. Students can steer a balloon in the following activity.

Procedure

Thread a long piece of string through a straw. Tie the ends of the string to two chairs. Then separate the chairs so that the string is stretched tight. Place the straw at one end of the string.

Blow up a balloon and seal it shut with string or a plastic bag twist tie. Tape the balloon to the straw threaded on the string.

Make sure nothing is in the way of the balloon's path, then untie the twist tie to release the air. The balloon will fly straight along the string.

Variation: Fasten one end of the string to an object higher than the chair so that the balloon's path will be upward, on an incline. Students can predict whether the balloon will travel farther this way. (Because of gravity the balloon will not travel as far.)

Rocket Propulsion, Part 3: Bag Rockets

Materials

- string
- straws
- lunch bags (1 for each student)
- yardstick or measuring tape
- balloons (small)
- markers/crayons
- tape
- Rocket Bar Graph black-line masters (1 for each student), page 39

This is a distance race. Have students use the Rocket Bar Graph blackline master on page 39 to record data.

Procedure

Have each student decorate his or her paper bag as desired. Tape a straw lengthwise onto the side of the bag. Thread the string through the straw, pull the string taut, and tie each end to chairs placed about six feet apart.

Have the children blow up their balloons and then fit the balloons into the bags, holding the balloons so that no air escapes. Then tell children to let go of the balloons. The "Bag Rockets" are forced forward on the string by propulsion (air rapidly escaping from the balloon).

When the balloons stop, have the students measure the distances covered. Let each child record his or her data on the board. Then they can use the Rocket Bar Graph blackline master for recording the class's data. Later, a large graph can be made showing the class results, along with written directions for making bag rockets, and a few finished samples.

Star Gazers:
A Constellation Peep Show

Materials

- paper towel rolls (1 for each child)

- tempera paint

- lined paper

- Constellation Information blackline master, page 40

- Constellation Templates blackline master, page 41

- straight pins

- aluminum foil

- corrugated cardboard (e.g., pieces cut from a supply box)

This project allows students to isolate one constellation and make a model of it for study.

Procedure

There are many myths related to constellations. Read some of these myths from resource books or from the information provided on page 40. Divide the chalkboard into sections. Record under the appropriate headings the facts the children recall from the myth about each constellation. (For example, Orion was a hunter, had two dogs, and was killed by a scorpion.)

Have the students choose a favorite constellation story and record the facts about it on their sheets of lined paper; set these aside. Using the tempera paint, have the children decorate the outside of their paper towel rolls (this can also be done ahead of time).

Place one of the Constellation Templates (page 41) on top of a piece of aluminum foil. Place both the template and the foil on top of the corrugated cardboard. With supervision, allow the students to prick the constellation pattern through the foil.

Carefully tape the foil over one end of the paper towel roll. Glue or tape the paper with the constellation facts onto the "Star Gazer." When students look through their gazers towards the light, they will be able to see their constellations.

Allow time for students to share their gazers and read one another's facts.

26

Connect the Stars to Make Your Own Constellations

Materials

- black construction paper (1 sheet for each child)

- pinto beans (any small bean or macaroni will do; you will need 7–10 for each child)

- gummed star stickers (7–10 for each child)

- chalk or white crayon

- lined paper (1 sheet for each child)

People of ancient cultures created pictures from the stars by imagining lines between them. They then made up stories about their "star picture" and why it was in the sky.

This creative writing activity allows the students the chance to make their own constellations. Before doing this activity, it may be helpful to read aloud some constellation stories. The "Star Gazer" activity is a good prerequisite to this one.

Procedure

Begin by reviewing the constellations that have been studied and the stories about them.

Pass out the black construction paper and 7–10 beans to each child. The children place the beans in one hand and then carefully drop them onto the paper from a height of about three inches. It is important that the beans be dropped randomly; the children should not place them in a determined order on their papers.

Pass out the gummed stickers. Tell children to use one of these to mark where each bean fell. This forms the child's constellation. At this point the beans can be collected.

Have the children study their star pictures, thinking of objects or scenes their constellations resemble. (Ask: "Does your constellation look like part of someone? Does it look like an animal?" and so on.)

Ask the children to name their constellations and tell a story about why it is in the sky. These stories can either be dictated to an adult helper or the teacher, or students can write them on their own. It may be appropriate to provide the students with a story frame such as the following: "This is Constellation _____ . It is in the sky because _____ . This is how it got up there—_____ ."

Stories can be shared and then displayed with the pictures.

Night and Day

Materials

- globe
- flashlight
- sticker, crayon, or chalk

By observing a model, students can more easily understand how the earth's position in relation to the sun creates day and night.

Procedure

Mark your location on the globe using the sticker, chalk, or crayon. Ask the children what the flashlight represents (the sun), and what the globe represents (the earth).

Darken the classroom and ask a volunteer to hold the flashlight. Rotate the globe from east to west so that the "sun" is shining in your location. Ask what time of day it is. Rotate the globe again so that your location is in the dark. Ask the children to infer the time again.

Go through the whole day, rotating the earth slowly and identifying the time of day.

Lunar Changes

Materials

■ 2 pieces of poster board

■ overhead projector or flashlight

■ marking pen

There are many myths and fantasy stories that explain why the moon appears to wax and wane. This exercise is designed to provide a visual model of the lunar changes in their relation to the earth and sun.

Procedure

Make a "moon" and "earth" out of the poster board and label each one with the marking pen. Have two student volunteers be the moon and the earth, respectively. Darken the room and use the overhead projector or the flashlight as the "sun" to shine light onto the "moon."

Next, have one child hold the "earth" and walk slowly between the projector or flashlight and the child holding the "moon." Stop the "earth" at intervals that illustrate the half and the quarter moon. Draw the different phases on the board as the exercise progresses.

Important Concepts:

1. Although we see the moon at night, it does not generate its own light. Rather, it reflects light from the sun.

2. When we see a full moon, it means that the sun and the moon are in a direct, uninterrupted line with one another.

Ideas for Discussion:

1. The moon goes through its cycle about once a month. The word *month* itself is from an Old English word *meno* which means "moon."

2. The rising and falling of the tides are caused by the moon's gravitational pull on the ocean.

3. The word *lunatic* is based on the word *lunar*. Many people believe that very strange behavior is more likely to occur during a full moon than at any other time.

Sun Dial Observation

Materials

- white paper plates (1 for each child)

- sharpened pencils (2 for each child)

For many children, time is an arbitrary, abstract concept. The sun dial observation project helps show time passing by recording the shadows cast by a pencil stuck into the ground.

Procedure

On a calm, sunny morning take the children to the schoolyard with their pencils and paper plates (make sure the children put their names or initials somewhere on the plate). Have each child make a sun dial by pushing the sharpened end of one of the pencils through the center of the plate, and then directly into the ground. The pencil serves as the "gnomon," which casts a shadow to tell time.

Have the children use the other pencil to trace the gnomon's shadow onto the paper plate sun dial.

Throughout the course of the day, have the children return several times to their sun dials to trace the pencil/gnomon's shadows with their other pencils. By the end of the exercise the paper plates will have pencil-drawn "spokes" radiating from their centers.

Follow-up: Have the students offer suggestions as to why the shadow moved. They may likely and logically say that the sun cast the different shadows as it moved across the sky. While the idea of movement is central to the concept of time, it is, of course, the earth that moves, not the sun. It may be necessary to provide the class with information about the earth's rotation (see item 3 under "Star Facts and Ideas for Discussion" on page 21).

String Clock

Materials

- string or light-colored yarn in 22-inch lengths (1 for each child)

- 2 different dark-colored markers

- glue

- Analog Clock blackline master (1 for each child), page 42

- Number Lines blackline master (1 for each child), page 43

- tape

Children sometimes have trouble learning to tell time by an analog clock because of its circular shape. We say that it is five after the hour when the minute hand is at the one. The String Clock lets the children count and mark the minutes between each number and then see them linearly for a more familiar view of counting.

Procedure

Starting at the 12 on the Analog Clock blackline master (page 42), put a dot of glue on each of the hour numbers. Also beginning at the 12, lay the string around the clock and allow time for the glue to dry. Use one of the markers to mark on the string at each of the hours. Use the other color to mark the string at each of the minutes.

Use the Number Lines blackline master (page 43) to make a number line of 60 minutes/12 hours. Students can make these themselves by cutting between the long solid lines and then taping or gluing the two strips together into one long strip. The Number Lines blackline master makes two number lines.

Gently pull the string off the clock and lay it straight across the number line. As a class, practice counting the minute marks. Also count by 5s (children often learn this very quickly).

Follow-up: It is important for the students to understand that the marks on the clock show the minutes, while the numbers represent the hours.

Overview of Blackline Masters

<u>Nursery Rhyme: Star Light, Star Bright</u>: See Day 1 of "Sharing Rhymes with the Class: A Basic Format," page x.

<u>Cloze Activity:</u> Partners take turns reading the rhymes, then determine which words complete the rhyme.

<u>Word Making: *-ar, -ay,* and *-ight* Words</u>: Children cut out the letters and put them together to make words that end with *ar, ay*, and *ight*.

<u>Rocket Bar Graph</u>: See Rocket Propulsion, Part 3, page 25.

<u>Constellation Information</u> and <u>Constellation Templates</u>: See "Star Gazers: A Constellation Peep Show," page 26.

<u>Analog Clock and Number Lines</u>: See "String Clock," page 31.

<u>Handwriting:</u> Children fill in the missing words, then trace the rhyme as a handwriting exercise.

<u>I Wish:</u> Students draw or write in the thought balloons things for which those animals might wish.

Star Light, Star Bright

Star light, star bright,
First star I see tonight—
I wish I may,
I wish I might
Have the wish
I wish tonight.

Star Light, Star Bright

Star light, star bright,
First star I see tonight—
I wish I may,
I wish I might
Have the wish
I wish tonight.

Star Light, Star Bright

Star light, star bright,
First star I see tonight—
I wish I may,
I wish I might
Have the wish
I wish tonight.

Star Light, Star Bright

Star light, star bright,
First star I see tonight—
I wish I may,
I wish I might
Have the wish
I wish tonight.

Name

Partner's Name

Star light, star bright,
First star I see tonight—
I wish I may,
I wish I might
Have the wish
I wish tonight.

Fill in the blanks:

Star light, _____ bright,

First star I see _____—

I _____ I may,

____ wish I might

Have the _____

I wish _____.

Cloze Activity

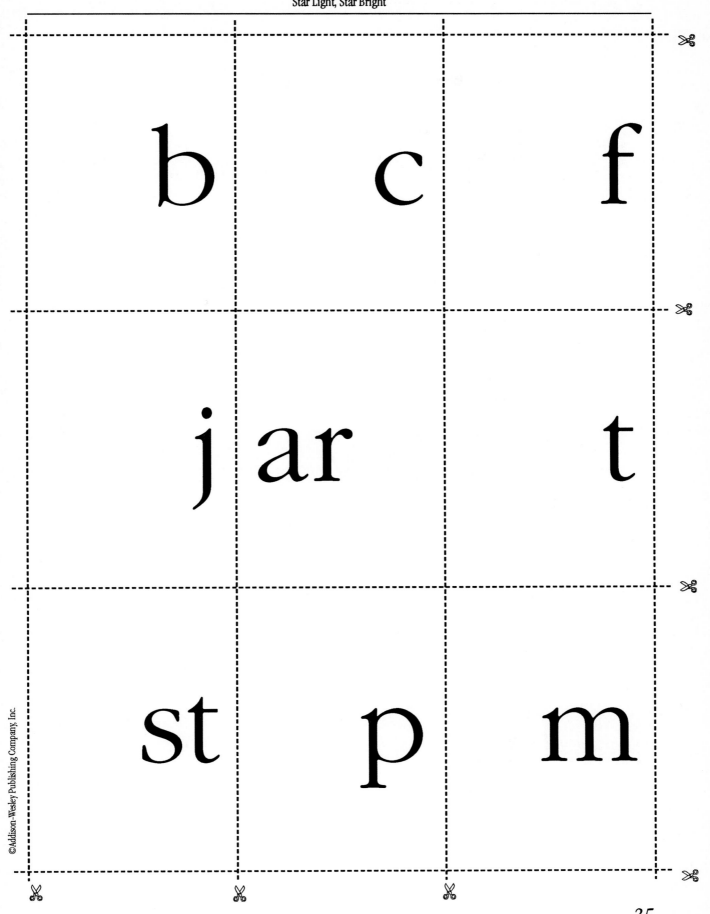

b c f

j ar t

st p m

Word Making: *-ar* Words

35

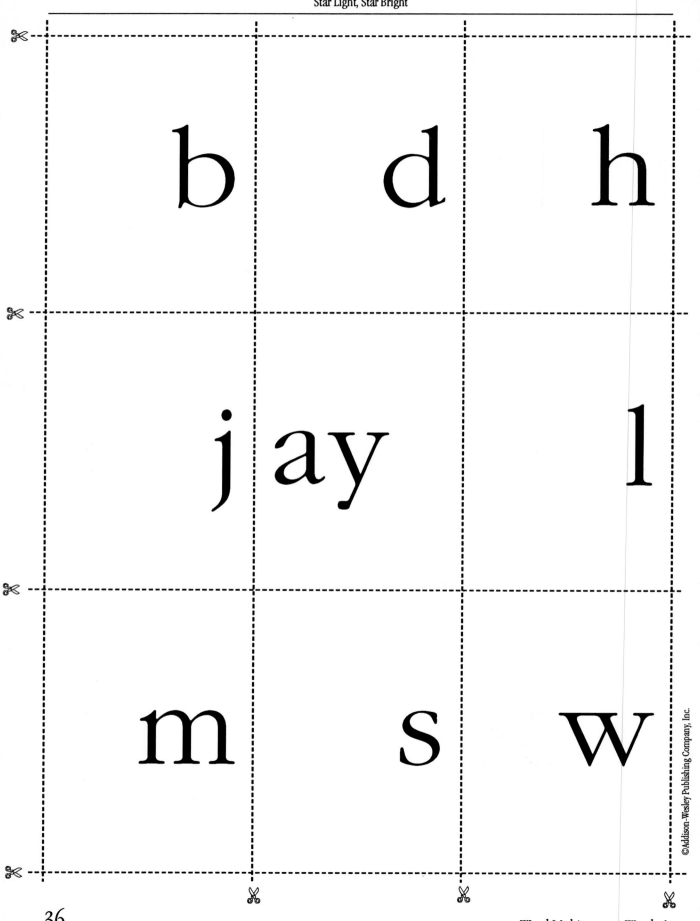

b   d   h

j ay   l

m   s   w

Word Making: *-ay* Words 1

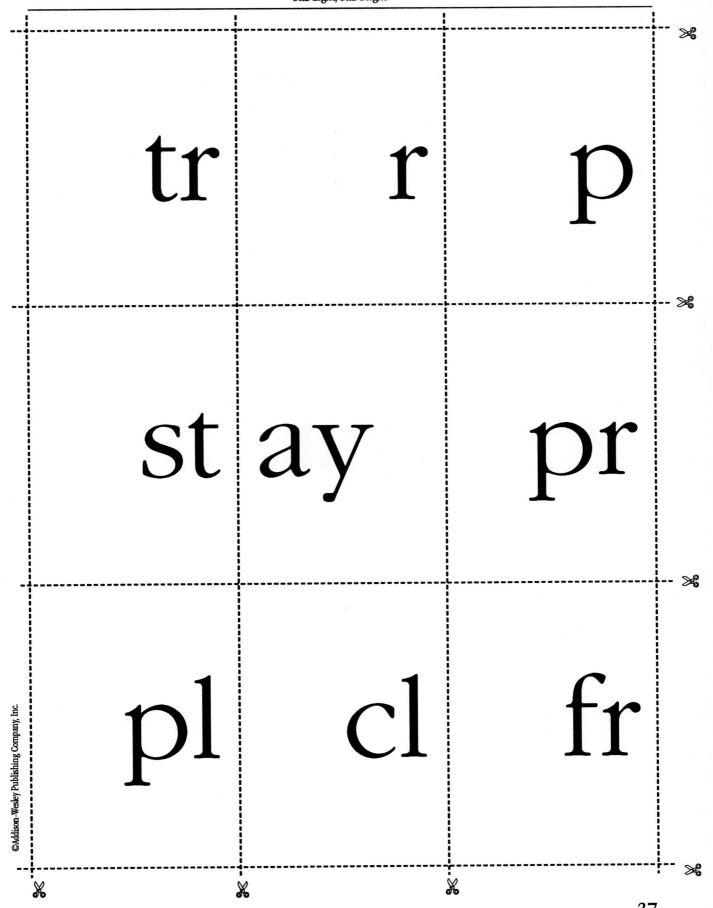

tr r p

st ay pr

pl cl fr

Word making: -*ay* Words 2

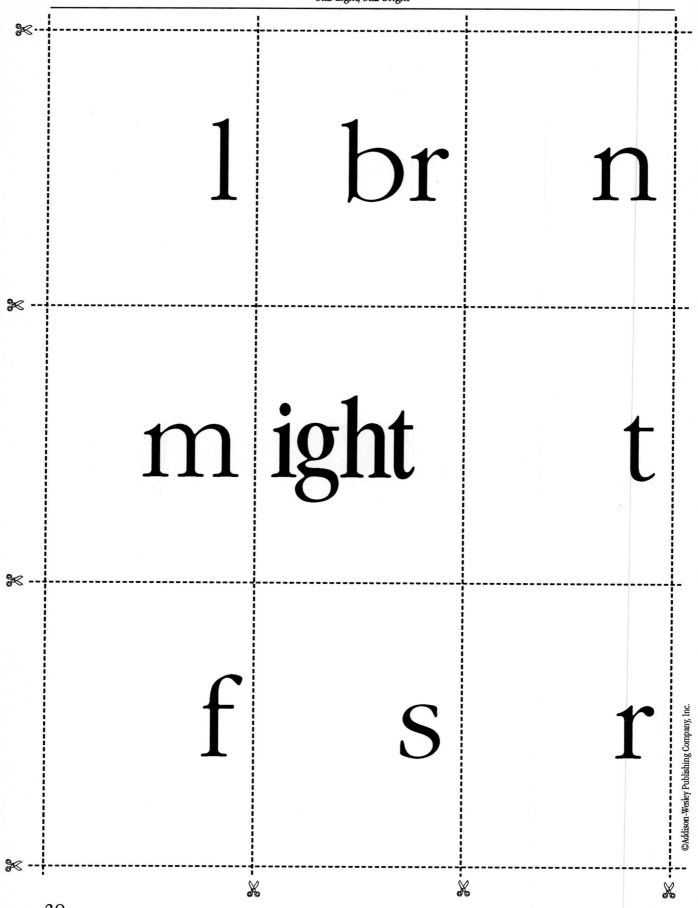

l   br   n

m ight   t

f   s   r

Word Making: *ight* Words

Name

Show how far the rockets went in Rocket Propulsion, Part 3.

Number of rockets

	1 Foot	1 1/2 Feet	2 Feet	2 1/2 Feet	3 Feet	3 1/2 Feet	4 Feet	4 1/2 Feet	5 Feet	5 1/2 Feet
20										
19										
18										
17										
16										
15										
14										
13										
12										
11										
10										
9										
8										
7										
6										
5										
4										
3										
2										
1										
0										

Distance Rockets Traveled

Rocket Bar Graph

Constellation Information

The Story of Orion

Orion was a hunter who always traveled with his two friends, Big Dog and Little Dog. Orion often bragged that he could kill any animal. A goddess named Juno became very angry because Orion was so boastful, and she sent a scorpion to kill him. The scorpion stung Orion's heel and he died.

Aesculapius, the best doctor in the world, was called to bring Orion back to life. Aesculapius claimed that he learned his secrets from snakes, and he always carried a snake with him. He did actually bring Orion back to life, which made the gods and goddesses very angry. One of them, Jupiter, threw a thunderbolt down and killed Orion and Aesculapius. If we look up in the sky at night we can see the scorpion, Aesculapius and his snake, and Orion and his two dogs.

Andromeda and the Great Whale

Andromeda was the beautiful daughter of Queen Cassiopeia and King Cepheus. Queen Cassiopeia told everyone that her daughter was beautiful—even more beautiful than the sea nymphs. Now the sea nymphs were goddesses and didn't like being compared with human beings. The sea god, Neptune, sent a great big whale to the shore of the King and Queen's land. There the whale ate many of their subjects. King Cepheus was very upset. How could he save his people? He was told that he would have to let the whale eat his beautiful daughter, Andromeda. So the girl was chained to a rock near the edge of the sea.

Perseus, who was very brave, could not stand to see this happen. Just as the whale jumped from the waves to eat Andromeda, Perseus killed it. He freed Andromeda, and the two were married and rode away on Pegasus, Perseus' winged horse.

Now if you look in the sky, you can see Queen Cassiopeia, with Andromeda, Perseus, Pegasus, the King, and the whale all close by.

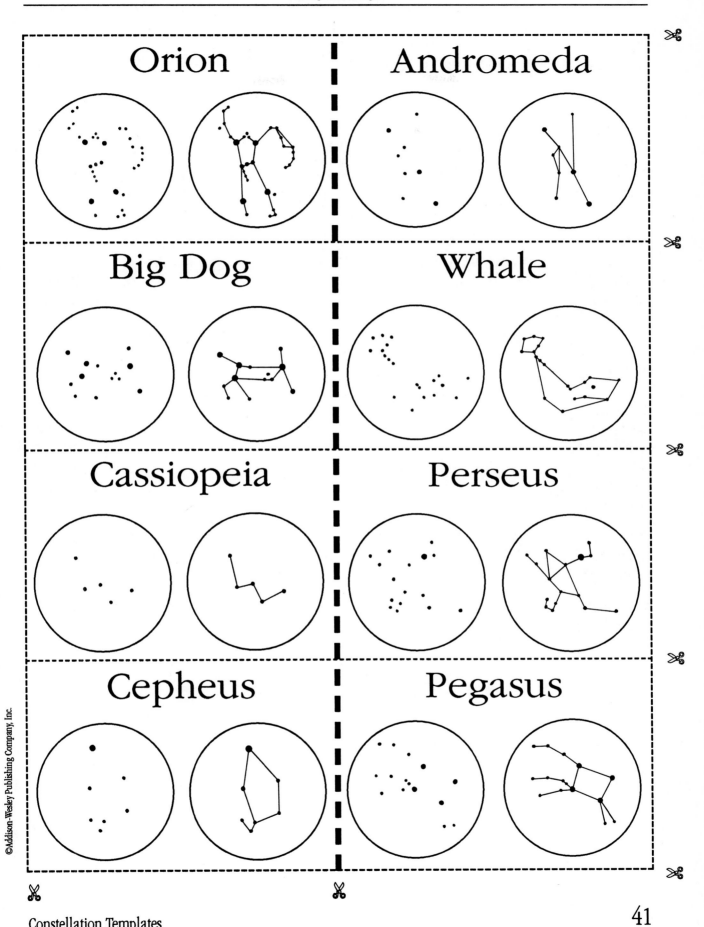

Orion

Andromeda

Big Dog

Whale

Cassiopeia

Perseus

Cepheus

Pegasus

Constellation Templates

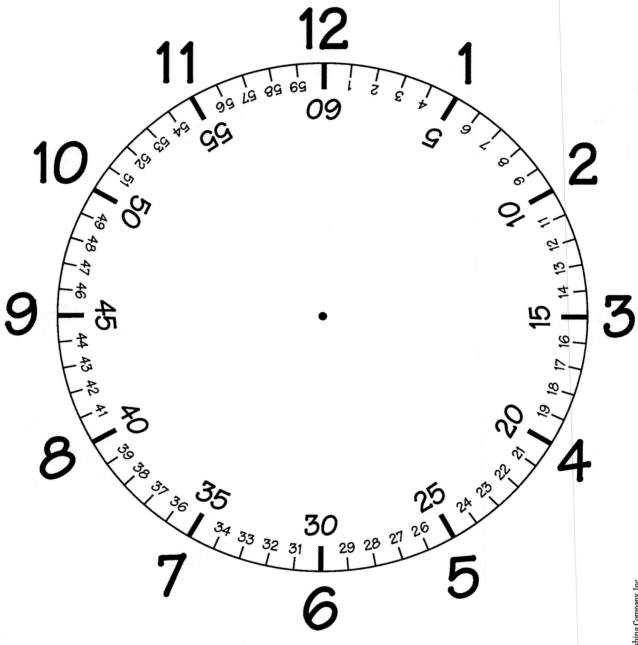

Analog Clock

©Addison-Wesley Publishing Company, Inc.

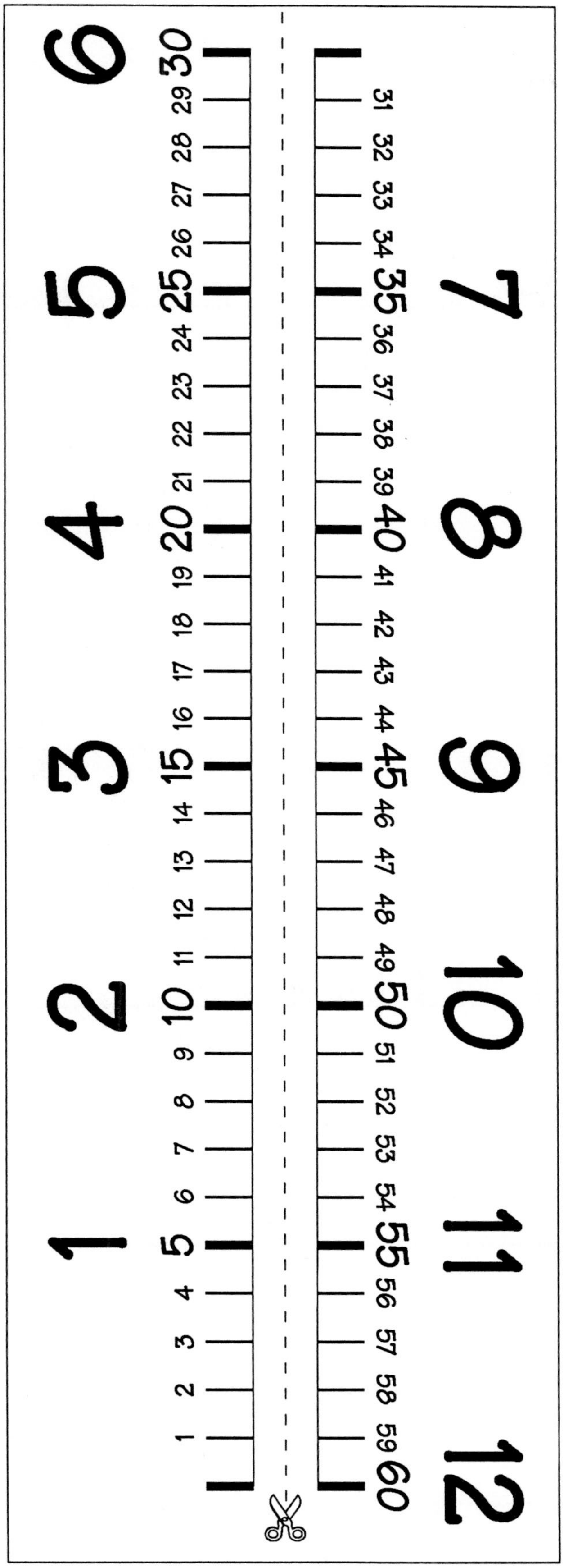

1 2 3 4 5 6 7 8 9 10 11 12
1 2 3 4 5 6 7 8 9 10 11 12 13 14 15 16 17 18 19 20 21 22 23 24 25 26 27 28 29 30
31 32 33 34 35 36 37 38 39 40 41 42 43 44 45 46 47 48 49 50 51 52 53 54 55 56 57 58 59 60

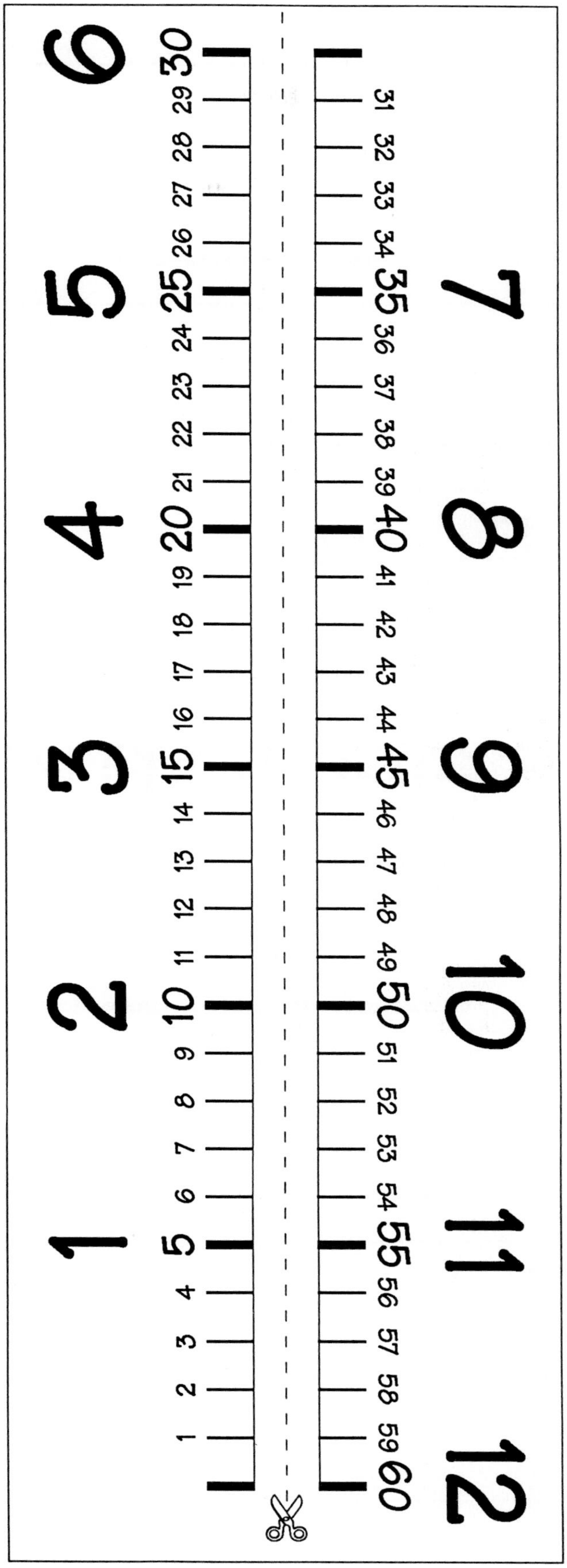

1 2 3 4 5 6 7 8 9 10 11 12
1 2 3 4 5 6 7 8 9 10 11 12 13 14 15 16 17 18 19 20 21 22 23 24 25 26 27 28 29 30
31 32 33 34 35 36 37 38 39 40 41 42 43 44 45 46 47 48 49 50 51 52 53 54 55 56 57 58 59 60

Name _____

Complete the rhyme by adding STAR or WISH in the correct blanks. Trace the rhyme.

_____ light,

_____ bright

First _____ I

see tonight---

I _____ I may,

I _____ I might

Have the _____

I _____ tonight.

Handwriting

Chapter Three

One, Two, Buckle My Shoe

One, two, buckle my shoe.
Three, four, shut the door.
Five, six, pick up sticks.
Seven, eight, lay them straight.
Nine, ten, do it again!

One, Two, Buckle My Shoe
Curriculum Web

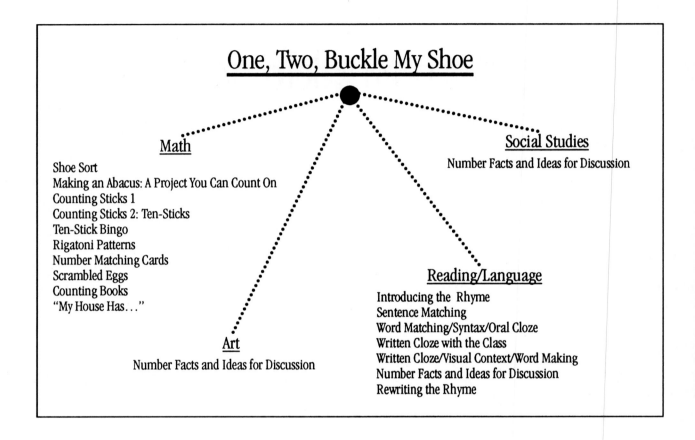

One, Two, Buckle My Shoe

Math

Shoe Sort
Making an Abacus: A Project You Can Count On
Counting Sticks 1
Counting Sticks 2: Ten-Sticks
Ten-Stick Bingo
Rigatoni Patterns
Number Matching Cards
Scrambled Eggs
Counting Books
"My House Has…"

Art

Number Facts and Ideas for Discussion

Social Studies

Number Facts and Ideas for Discussion

Reading/Language

Introducing the Rhyme
Sentence Matching
Word Matching/Syntax/Oral Cloze
Written Cloze with the Class
Written Cloze/Visual Context/Word Making
Number Facts and Ideas for Discussion
Rewriting the Rhyme

Related Literature

One Sun: A Book of Terse Verse, by Bruce McMillan (Holiday, 1990)

One, Two, One Pair, by Bruce McMillan (Scholastic, 1991)

Ten, Nine, Eight, by Molly Bang (Greenwillow, 1983)

Number Facts and Ideas for Discussion

1. Reading "One, Two, Buckle My Shoe" gives children practice in counting and reading numbers in English. Your class may be interested in learning how to count in other languages as well. The following lists show words for numbers 1–10 in German, Spanish, and Swahili. Students (or their parents) may be able to teach the class how to count in other languages.

GERMAN	SPANISH	SWAHILI
eins (eyenss)	uno (OO-no)	moja (MO-jah)
zwei (tsveye)	dos (dohss)	mbili (m-BEE-lee)
drei (dreye)	tres (trayss)	tatu (TA-too)
vier (feer)	quatro (KWAH-tro)	nne (N-nay)
funf (fewnf)	cinco (SEEN-ko)	tano (TAH-no)
sechs (zehks)	seis (sayss)	sita (SEE-tah)
sieben (ZEEB-en)	siete (SYAY-tay)	saba (SAH-bah)
acht (ahkht)	ocho (O-cho)	nane (NAH-nay)
neun (noyn)	nueve (NWAY-vay)	tisa (TEE-sah)
zehn (tsayn)	diez (dyess)	kumi (KOO-mee)

2. There are many variations to the "nine, ten" couplet of this rhyme. We've used "Nine, ten, do it again!" Other versions include:

> Nine, ten, Nine, ten
> A big, fat hen! A big, red hen!

As a class, brainstorm other ways to end this rhyme (for example, "Nine, ten, pigs in a pen!"). After brainstorming, you may want to list all of the ending words separately on the board (*ten, hen, pen,* and so on) and ask children to comment on their similarities and differences. It will be interesting to note that all of the words rhyme, and most end in *-en,* but *again* ends differently.

3. Our version of this nursery rhyme ends with ten; other versions of the same rhyme continue on to twenty. Children can explore other nursery rhyme books for other variations.

4. In this rhyme, children read about buckling shoes, closing doors, picking up sticks and laying them straight. To develop vocabulary, ask the class or groups of students to brainstorm answers to the following questions. Make lists on the chalkboard of the words they suggest.

> What else can you buckle?
> What else do you shut?
> What else do you pick up?

Children can record answers on the "One, Two" blackline master on page 67.

5. The largest named number is called "googol"— it is 1 followed by a hundred zeros: 10,000,000,000,000,000,000,000,000,000, 000,000,000,000,000,000,000,000,000,000, 000,000,000,000,000,000,000,000,000,000, 000.

It was named by mathematician Edward Krasner's young nephew, who was asked what he would call a very large number.

6. Use counting as a way to help children get ready. Young children often don't know what it means to be ready to go in "one minute." Counting aloud for them helps them realize the impending deadline while reinforcing number patterns (for example: "you need to be cleaned up by the time I count to 100 by fives: 5, 10, 15 . . ." or, "Finish up by the time I count down to zero: 10, 9, 8, . . .").

7. Reproduce the "My House Has. . ." blackline master on page 84 and give each child a copy. Have children take the sheet home and fill in the number of each item they have in their house.

Shoe Sort

Materials

- 1 photocopied shoe for each child from the Shoes for Class Graph blackline master, page 68

- 1 large graph made on chart or butcher paper (see the Shoe Sort Graph blackline master, page 69, for an example)

Graphs help children learn to categorize and count. Students become involved in this activity by using their own shoes as a graphing subject.

Procedure

Show children the graph. Talk about the different ways shoes can fasten. Ask all the children with slip-on shoes to stand up; then have those whose shoes touch-fasten stand; next, those whose shoes tie, and finally those whose shoes buckle. Try fitting each category into the rhyme (for example, "One, two, slip on your shoe").

Give each child a shoe from the photocopied blackline master on page 68. Students should write their names on the front, then color the shoe to match their own.

Let each child glue his or her paper shoe in the appropriate column to make a shoe graph.

Study the graph as a class, and have the children make observations. These can be recorded next to the graph. Children might say, for example:

"Two people have shoes that tie."

"More people use Velcro."

"Only one person buckles her shoes."

Extension: Photocopy a Shoe Sort Graph for each child. Students can either fill in the graph to match the class graph or take it home, poll family members, and make their own graphs.

One, Two Relays

Do this relay right before recess or on a rainy day when the children can't play outside. It is not a quiet activity.

Procedure

Designate two time keepers and a time recorder. Have everyone line up near the door to the room. Put the students' names on the board in the order in which they are standing in line. Clear away the desks if necessary. Have each runner open the door before starting. Walk through the course to model the procedure. The children say the rhyme as the runner is at each point. Have everyone unfasten his or her shoe.

CLASS SAYS:	RUNNER:
One, two, buckle my shoe	• fastens his or her shoe
Three, four, shut the door	• shuts the door
Five, six, pick up sticks	• picks up the ice cream sticks
Seven, eight, lay them straight	• lays them end to end on the floor or on a desk
Nine, ten, do it again	• runs back to the beginning and taps next runner to go

At this point the time keeper calls out the time to the time recorder, who puts it on the board next to that person's name. Continue the relay until everyone has had a chance.

Allow some cool-down time by examining the different times listed on the board.

Variation: Instead of a relay, have children do a "walk through" of the rhyme. To make a "walk through," you will need a large strip of butcher paper and 10 shoe-shaped footprints (5 left feet and 5 right feet) cut from

One, Two Relays (continued)

construction paper. Hold the butcher paper longways, and at one end of the strip glue two footprints (a left print and a right print) a step apart. Place a number 1 on the first footprint and a 2 on the second. Directly above the prints, write "Buckle my shoe" on the butcher paper. Glue down steps 3 and 4, writing "Shut the door" above them. Continue adding steps and lines from the rhyme until the rhyme is complete. Students walk through the rhyme by stepping on the footprints and pantomiming the action.

Making an Abacus:
A Project You Can Count On

Materials

■ heavy wire coat hangers (1 for each abacus you plan to make)

■ beads in 2 colors, 5 of each color for each abacus (If beads are too expensive or not available you may use dyed rigatoni or some similarly shaped pasta. See Rigatoni Patterns, page 58, for dyeing information. The abacus will be less sturdy but will still work.)

■ wire cutters

■ pliers

■ duct or electrician's tape

A tool such as the abacus helps children who are in the concrete stage of development visualize the meaning of counting. Because of the sharp objects used, this is a project for the teacher or adult volunteers to make for the children to use.

Procedure

1. Use the wire cutters to snip off the hook part of the hanger.
2. Use the pliers to bend one side of the hanger into a triangle with 2 1/4-inch sides.
3. Loop the end of the hanger over the side.
4. Tape the end to protect the children from its sharp point.
5. Straighten out the rest of the hanger enough so that you can thread the beads or macaroni on it. Put on five beads of one color, then five of the other color.
6. Use the pliers to make a triangle as in (2) and (3) on the other end of the hanger wire.

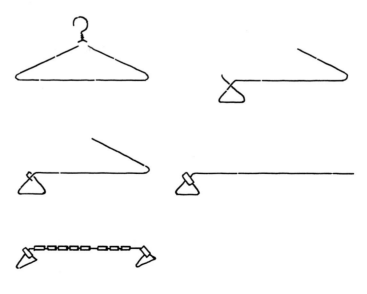

Counting Sticks 1

Materials

- ice cream sticks (10 for each child)

- oat cereal or any dry cereal with small, firm bits

- small cups (1 for every 2 students)

- glue

- construction paper, cut into squares (approx. 4 by 4 inches)

- small self-sealing plastic bags (1 for each student)

- paper for recording results

- Math Sticks blackline master (1 for each student), page 70

Young children need to manipulate materials in order to grasp basic counting and addition concepts. During this activity, students practice counting as they make the materials. Then they manipulate the materials to find the combination for a given sum.

Procedure

Give each child 10 ice cream sticks. Pour cereal bits into cups and distribute one cup to every 2 students.

Give each pair of students a paper square. Pour glue onto the square.

Each student will make a number set representing 0-9 by leaving the first stick empty (this is 0), dipping a cereal bit in glue and placing it at the top of a stick to represent 1, gluing 2 bits on the next stick, and so on until 1 through 9 have been represented.

Students use their sets to represent a particular sum. For example, if the sum is 8, children can lay out the 5-stick and the 3-stick, then record 5 + 3 = 8. They should then try to make more combinations that equal 8, such as 6 and 2, or 8 and 0. At first, students may work in pairs, with the whole class working on the same number. Later, sums can be written on cards and randomly distributed to students.

Counting sticks can be stored in the plastic bags. Use the Math Sticks blackline master on page 70 for seatwork or homework.

Variation: Lima beans may be used instead of counting sticks to find combinations for a particular sum. Spray paint large dry lima beans with a bright color on one side, leaving the other side white. Give students a number, and have them count that many beans into a cup. Tell them to spill the beans onto the table and record the number of beans that are color side up, then the number of beans that are white side up. This creates a number sentence (for example, if a child counts 3 colored and 4 white, she or he would record 3 + 4 = 7). Children can try for as many different combinations as they can get.

Counting Sticks 2: Ten-Sticks

Materials

- ice cream sticks (10 for each child)

- oat cereal (as described in Counting Sticks 1)

- small cups (1 for every 2 students)

- small self-sealing plastic bags

- glue

- construction paper cut into squares (approx. 4 by 4 inches)

This activity provides hands-on counting experience as children make manipulatives for use during math.

Procedure

Give each child 10 ice cream sticks. Pour cereal into the cups. Distribute one cup to every two students.

Give each pair of students a construction paper square. Pour glue onto the square.

Students dip a cereal bit into the glue, then place it on the ice cream stick. Students will need to place 10 bits on each stick.

When a student is done with a stick, the partner checks it by counting the number of bits to make sure there are 10. The stick is then put aside to dry.

When all of the sticks are completed and dry, students should put 10 sticks into each plastic bag. They will also need to add 9 loose cereal bits to each bag. These materials can then be used during math for the following counting activities:

Game 1: Give each child (or each pair of children) a bag of materials. Explain that each stick means 10, because there are 10 cereal bits on it. Demonstrate how to represent different numbers using the sticks and loose bits (to model, you might want to draw large versions of sticks and bits on the board, or make transparency models for the overhead projector). For instance, to make 12, students would lay out 1 stick and 2 cereal bits. Explain that the digit 1 in 12 represents the ten-stick, and the digit 2 represents the 2 loose cereal bits.

Call out numbers and ask students to illustrate those numbers using their materials. In the beginning, call out numbers up to 19; as students

Counting Sticks 2:
Ten-Sticks (continued)

gain more experience with higher numbers, you can gradually show them how to illustrate 20, 30, and so on. Some students will be able to count above 10. For example: to make 14, they will lay down 1 stick, then count on by saying "11, 12, 13, 14" as they count out the cereal bits. Other children will need to count out each bit on the stick first. As they gain more practice, they will eventually be able to count on from 10.

This game can be followed up with the Ten-Stick Math blackline master on page 70.

Game 2: Divide students into groups of 4. Give each player a bag of materials, and each group one small cup and a die. Players empty their bags by piling all of the ten-sticks in the middle of the table, and putting all loose cereal bits in the cup in the center of the table.

Players take turns rolling the die. They take the number of cereal bits indicated on the die from the cup (for instance, if they roll a 5, they may take 5 bits). When 10 bits have been accumulated, a player may trade them in for a ten-stick. The first player to reach 50 (or 100, if time permits) is the winner.

Players return materials to the center of the table, then refill their bags with 10 ten-sticks and 9 loose cereal bits.

Ten-Stick Bingo

- Ten-Stick Bingo Card blackline masters (pages 71–78), reproduced and cut along the double lines to make 4 cards from each sheet (The 8 blackline masters at the end of the chapter provide 32 different cards. For greater durability, laminate the cards.)

- 9 bingo markers for each player (plastic chips or small squares of paper)

- 1–30 Bingo Pieces blackline master, page 79 (reproduced, cut into individual numbers, and stored in an envelope)

- Ten-Stick Bingo Master Sheet, page 80

- envelope

Math drills are more interesting for children when they are presented in a game format. Ten-Stick Bingo is a place-value drill using nine-square bingo cards, which can be recycled among the students.

Procedure

This game is played just like regular Bingo. Pass out a Ten-Stick Bingo Card and nine place markers to each student. Pull out a number from the envelope and call it. Have the students put a marker on the square that represents the number called. (As you call each number, place it on your master sheet to make checking the winners easier.) The first student to get three squares in a horizontal, vertical, or diagonal row wins the game. Check the winning numbers against the master sheet.

Variations:

1. Blackout Bingo: Winner must have all nine squares on the card covered.

2. Frame Bingo: Winner must have the eight perimeter squares on the card covered.

Rigatoni Patterns

Materials

- rigatoni (1 pound for each color desired—we recommend 4 pounds)
- food coloring
- rubbing alcohol
- newspaper
- large bowl
- wooden spoon

Children enjoy creating their own patterns. In this activity, students use dyed rigatoni to make a pattern, then record the patterns with crayons on the accompanying blackline master.

Part I—Dyeing the Rigatoni (for teachers)

Procedure

Pour 1/2 cup of alcohol into the large bowl. Add several drops of food coloring to the alcohol and swirl to combine. Gently pour the rigatoni into the bowl and stir with the wooden spoon until the rigatoni takes on the color of the food coloring. Carefully lay the dyed rigatoni in one layer on the newspaper and let them dry. Repeat the procedure for each color.

Materials

- dyed rigatoni
- small buckets or similar containers to hold the rigatoni
- yarn cut into 24-inch lengths with tape around one end to act as a needle
- Rigatoni Patterns blackline master (1 for each child), page 81
- crayons

Part II—Making the Patterns (this activity works well in a learning center)

Procedure

Discuss the fact that a pattern is a repeating series. Show children how to string the rigatoni on the yarn. Have them tie a piece of rigatoni around the end of the yarn that is not taped, then use the taped end to string various colors of rigatoni to make a pattern. Have the children record the pattern by coloring in one row on the Rigatoni Patterns blackline master, page 81. Then they may take the rigatoni off the yarn and make a new pattern. Let the children make several different patterns, recording each on the worksheet.

At the end of the unit the children may make one final pattern, then tie the yarn ends together to make a necklace to take home.

Number Matching Cards

Materials

- Number Matching Cards blackline master (1 for each student), page 82

- oaktag cut into 2 1/4-by-5 1/2-inch pieces (2 for each student)

- hole punch

- glue

- scissors

- yarn or string cut into 36-inch lengths

These Number Matching Cards are easy to make, fun to use, and self-correcting. This project gives children practice in matching the numerals with their word names.

Procedure

Cut out the card along the dotted black line. Fold along the center line, then lay open. Sandwich oaktag inside the cards, then glue it in place. Let dry.

Cut out the triangles on both sides and punch a hole in the top of the card. (Children may need help with the hole punch.) Thread a yarn piece through the hole and double knot it.

Repeat the procedure for the second card.

Show the children how to start:

1. Bring the length of yarn from behind the card, through the notch of the first number on the left side.

2. Stretch the yarn across the front and through the notch next to the name of that number (Example: *4* to *four*).

3. Stretch the yarn across the back and pull it up through the notch of the next number on the left.

4. Continue to work the yarn back and forth in the order of the numbers as they appear from top to bottom on the left side of the card.

If students have matched the numbers correctly, they will see their yarn match all the lines drawn on the back of the card.

Scrambled Eggs

Materials

- egg cartons (1 for each game you want to make)

- black marker

- index cards (12 for each game) or heavy oaktag cut into 3-by-5-inch pieces

- 2 one-pound bags of white navy beans

- glue

- Numbers blackline masters (1 master will make 2 games), page 83

- paper cup (1 for each game)

In this game children work with a partner to practice numbers and their corresponding word names.

Procedure

Divide the group into teams of two. Give each team an egg carton and a copy of the Numbers blackline master (page 83). Have them cut out the labels with the number words only, scramble them, and then glue one number word in each egg carton cup.

Pass out the index cards and cups filled with beans. Have the children cut out the labels with numerals and written names, glue one onto each of the index cards, and then glue the corresponding number of navy beans onto the card.

To Play: The partners sit facing each other, one with the egg carton and paper cup of beans. The other partner calls out a number and the child with the egg carton finds the written number and puts the appropriate number of beans in that section of the carton.

When all the numbers have been called, the partners check the work together by counting the beans in each section. After checking, the two exchange jobs and play again.

Counting Books

Materials

■ camera

■ photo album or small book with pages numbered 1–10 (in numeral and word form)

This activity gives students practice counting things in their environment.

Procedure

Divide the class into ten small groups. Assign each group a number from 1 to 10. Each group will be responsible for finding an item or items for a page in the book. For example, Group 4 will need to agree on four items that are alike (e.g., four pencils, four children, or four books).

Take a picture of the item set chosen by the children. When the photos have been developed, children can place them along with their names on the proper page in the book. The result will be a counting book full of items from the classroom environment.

Extension: Set up a book-making center with small books (with pages numbered from 1 to 10), magazines, and glue. Children can cut and glue pictures from the magazines to make their own counting books.

Rewriting the Rhyme

Materials

■ chart paper

■ chalkboard or other area for recording the group's responses

This nursery rhyme provides a meaningful context in which students can explore rhyming patterns. By rewriting each line, students get practice developing rhyming words. (This activity works well with Ideas for Discussion number 2.)

Procedure

Provide students with the following frame:

One, two,_____

Three, four,_____

Five, six, _____

Seven, eight, _____

Nine, ten, _____

As a group, brainstorm ways to fill in each line. Discuss why some words fit and others do not (for example, why "One, two, go to the zoo" sounds better than "One two, row the boat").

Make a class big book of the new rhyme.

Extension: Provide materials for individual students or small groups to make personal rhyme books. You will need to provide small books, writing and drawing tools, and a copy of the rhyme frame for reference. Students can use the rhyme developed by the class, or make up their own.

Overview of Blackline Masters

Nursery Rhyme: One Two, Buckle My Shoe: See Day 1 of "Sharing Rhymes with the Class: A Basic Format," page x.

Cloze Activity: Partners take turns reading the rhymes, then determine which words complete the rhyme.

Word Making: -en Words: Children cut out the letters and put them together to make words that end with en.

One, Two: See Ideas for Discussion number 4 (page 48); also appropriate for homework.

Shoes for Class Graph: See "Shoe Sort" activity, page 50.

Shoe Sort Graph: See "Shoe Sort" activity, page 50.

Math Sticks : See "Counting Sticks 1 and 2," pages 54–56.

Ten-Stick Bingo Cards: Use with Ten-Stick Bingo Game, page 57.

1–30 Bingo Pieces: Use with Ten-Stick Bingo Game, page 57.

Ten-Stick Bingo Master Sheet: Use with Ten-Stick Bingo Game, page 57.

Rigatoni: See Rigatoni Patterns activity, page 58.

Number Matching Cards: See Number Matching Cards activity, page 59.

Numbers: See Scrambled Eggs activity, page 60.

My House Has . . .: Have the children take this page home for homework and fill in the number of each item they have at home.

Handwriting: Children fill in the missing words, then trace the the rhyme as a handwriting exercise. Reproduce pages 85 and 86 back to back.

Book to Illustrate: Reproduce back to back pages 87, 88 and pages 89, 90. Have the students fold the book in half, staple it into book form, and then illustrate it. Illustrating requires that the children read and understand the text. Subsequently, their own illustrations serve as context clues when they reread the rhyme.

One, Two

One, two, buckle my shoe.

Three, four, shut the door.

Five, six, pick up sticks.

Seven, eight, lay them straight.

Nine, ten, do it again!

One, Two

One, two, buckle my shoe.

Three, four, shut the door.

Five, six, pick up sticks.

Seven, eight, lay them straight.

Nine, ten, do it again!

One, Two

One, two, buckle my shoe.

Three, four, shut the door.

Five, six, pick up sticks.

Seven, eight, lay them straight.

Nine, ten, do it again!

One, Two

One, two, buckle my shoe.

Three, four, shut the door.

Five, six, pick up sticks.

Seven, eight, lay them straight.

Nine, ten, do it again!

Nursery Rhyme

Name_____

Partner's Name_____

One, two, buckle my shoe.
Three, four, shut the door.
Five, six, pick up sticks.
Seven, eight, lay them straight.
Nine, ten, do it again!

Fill in the blanks:

One, two, buckle my _____.

Three, _____, shut the door.

Five, six, pick up _____.

Seven, _____, lay them straight.

Nine, ten, do it _____!

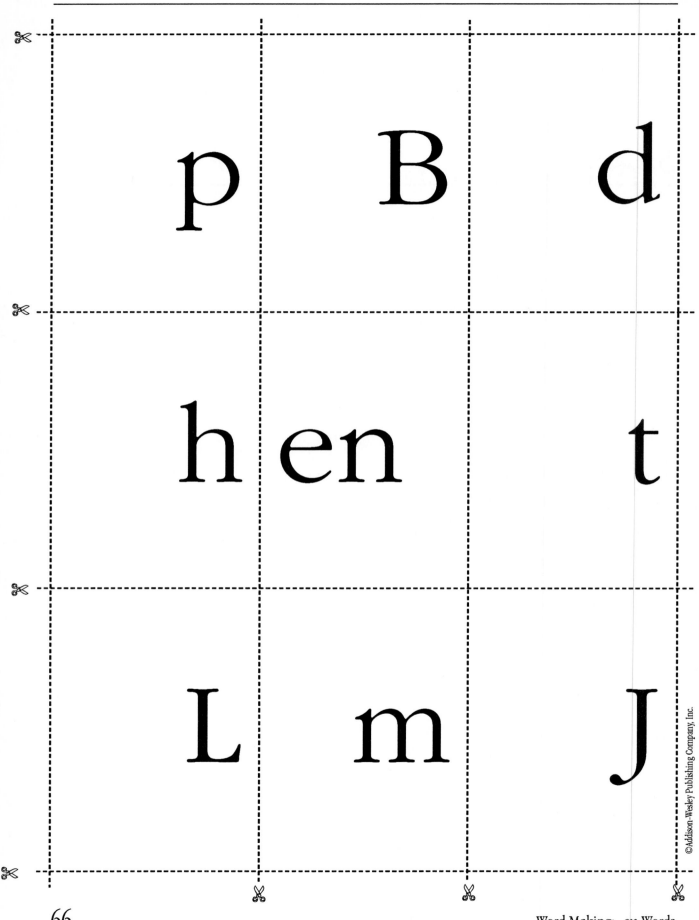

p   B   d

h en   t

L   m   J

Word Making: *-en* Words

Name _____

| One,
two,
buckle
my
shoe.
★ ★
★ What else
do you
buckle? | Three,
four,
shut
the
door.
★ ★ ★
What else
do you
shut? | Five,
six,
pick up
sticks.
★ ★ ★
What else
do you
pick up? | Seven,
eight,
lay
them
straight.
★ ★ ★
What else
do you lay
straight? | Nine,
ten,
do it
again!
★ ★
★ What else
do you do
again? |

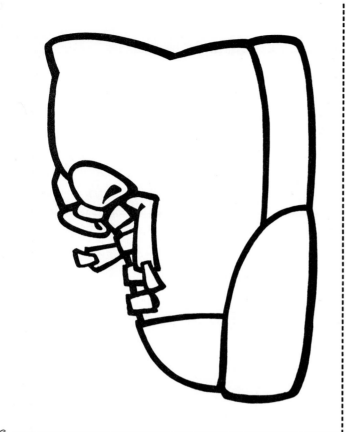

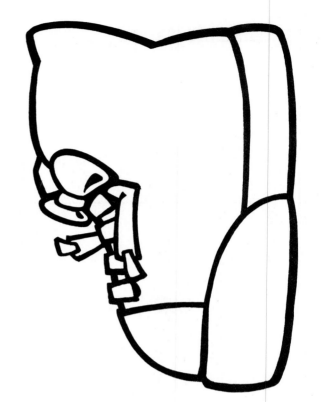

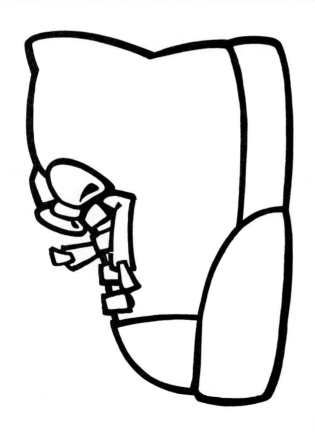

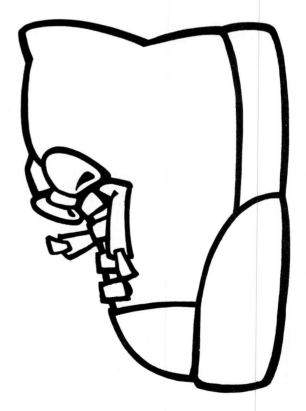

Shoes for Class Graph

Name _____

Show what kinds of shoes the
children in your class have on.

11 —

10 —

9 —

8 —

7 —

6 —

5 —

4 —

3 —

2 —

1 —

Shoe Sort Graph

_____ + _____ = _____

_____ + _____ = _____

_____ + _____ = _____

_____ + _____ = _____

_____ + _____ = _____

_____ + _____ = _____

_____ + _____ = _____

_____ + _____ = _____

_____ + _____ = _____

_____ + _____ = _____

_____ + _____ = _____

_____ + _____ = _____

Math Sticks

Ten-Stick Bingo Card 1

Ten-Stick Bingo Card 2

Ten-Stick Bingo Card 3

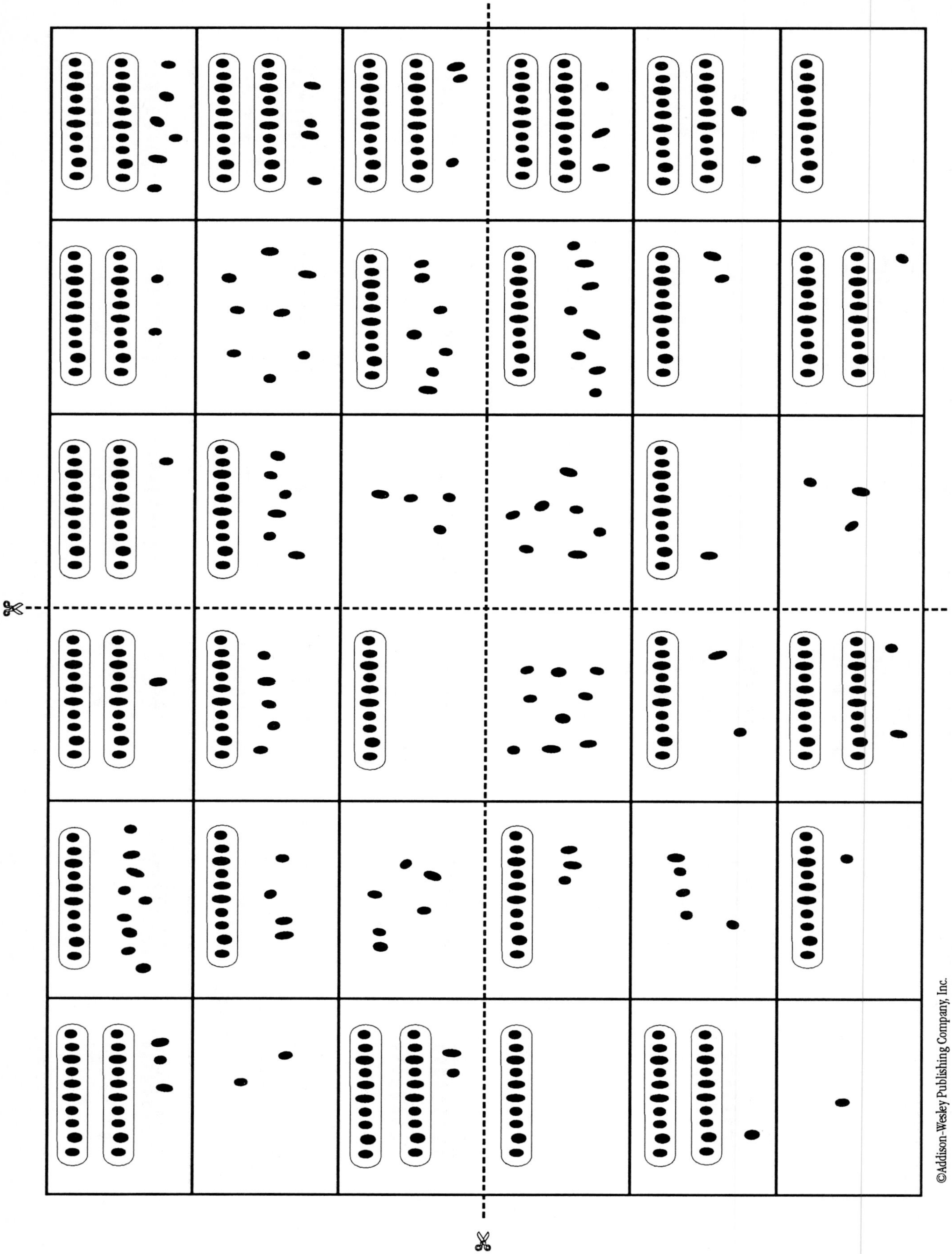

Ten-Stick Bingo Card 5

Ten-Stick Bingo Card 6

Ten-Stick Bingo Card 7

Ten-Stick Bingo Card 8

©Addison-Wesley Publishing Company, Inc.

Cut out numbers and put in bag or envelope to draw for "Ten-Stick Bingo."

1	2	3	4	5	6
7	8	9	10	11	12
13	14	15	16	17	18
19	20	21	22	23	24
25	26	27	28	29	30

1–30 Bingo Pieces

1	2	3	4	5	6
7	8	9	10	11	12
13	14	15	16	17	18
19	20	21	22	23	24
25	26	27	28	29	30

Ten-Stick Bingo Master Sheet

RIGATONI PATTERNS

Rigatoni Patterns

4	six
1	one
2	four
6	two
3	five
5	three

fold

11	eight
8	twelve
9	seven
12	eleven
7	ten
10	nine

ONE | TWO | THREE | FOUR | FIVE | SIX | SEVEN | EIGHT | NINE | TEN | ELEVEN | TWELVE

1 | 2 | 3 | 4 | 5 | 6 | 7 | 8 | 9 | 10 | 11 | 12

one | two | three | four | five | six | seven | eight | nine | ten | eleven | twelve

---

ONE | TWO | THREE | FOUR | FIVE | SIX | SEVEN | EIGHT | NINE | TEN | ELEVEN | TWELVE

1 | 2 | 3 | 4 | 5 | 6 | 7 | 8 | 9 | 10 | 11 | 12

one | two | three | four | five | six | seven | eight | nine | ten | eleven | twelve

My house has...

_____ chairs　　_____ beds　　_____tables

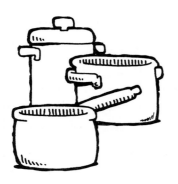  

_____ pots　　_____ spoons　　_____ lamps

_____ stairs　　_____ people

Name _____ Fill in the blanks and trace the rhyme.

One, _____,

Buckle my shoe.

Three, _____,

Shut the door.

Five, _____,

Pick up sticks.

Seven, _____,

Lay them straight.

Handwriting, page 1

85

Name_____

Nine, _____,

Do it again!

One, Two

Illustrated by:_____

One, two, buckle my shoe.

2

Three, four, shut the door.

3

Nine, ten, do it again!

6

Seven, eight, lay them straight.

5

Five, six, pick up sticks.

4

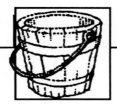

Chapter Four

Jack and Jill

Jack and Jill
Went up the hill
To fetch a pail of water.

Jack fell down
And broke his crown
And Jill came tumbling after.

Jack and Jill Curriculum Web

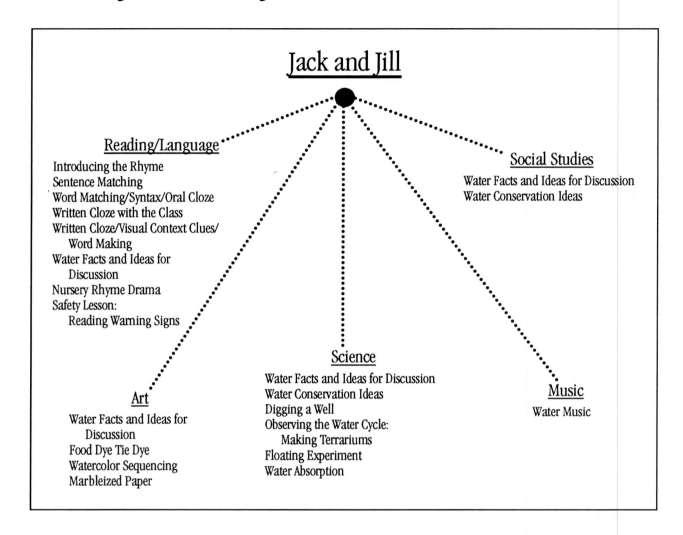

Jack and Jill

Reading/Language
Introducing the Rhyme
Sentence Matching
Word Matching/Syntax/Oral Cloze
Written Cloze with the Class
Written Cloze/Visual Context Clues/
    Word Making
Water Facts and Ideas for
    Discussion
Nursery Rhyme Drama
Safety Lesson:
    Reading Warning Signs

Social Studies
Water Facts and Ideas for Discussion
Water Conservation Ideas

Art
Water Facts and Ideas for
    Discussion
Food Dye Tie Dye
Watercolor Sequencing
Marbleized Paper

Science
Water Facts and Ideas for Discussion
Water Conservation Ideas
Digging a Well
Observing the Water Cycle:
    Making Terrariums
Floating Experiment
Water Absorption

Music
Water Music

Related Literature

Curious George Goes to the Hospital, by Margaret and H.G. Rey (Houghton Mifflin Co., 1966)

The Magic Schoolbus at the Waterworks, by Joanna Cole (Scholastic, 1988)

Water Facts and Ideas for Discussion

1. Take advantage of a rainy day to make some observations. Are the raindrops hitting the classroom window? Why or why not? If they are not, is there another window in the school that they are hitting? After the rain has stopped, take a walk outside. Where are the biggest puddles? Why do you think the puddles are there instead of somewhere else?

2. Some substances, such as salt, dissolve in water. The result is called a solution. Other substances, such as sand, will not dissolve. Sand and water are called a mixture.

   Have the children try stirring a spoonful of salt into a clear glass or plastic cup of water. Next, have them stir a spoonful of sand into a cup of water. Ask for their observations about what they see in each cup.

3. Most liquids will mix with water, but some will not. Add 1/4 cup of milk to 1 cup of water. The milk will mix with the water, making it cloudy white. Ask the children to tell you what they see. Next, add 1/4 cup of oil to 1 cup of water (a colored oil, such as yellow cooking oil, works better than clear oil because the children can see it better). The oil will float in large globules to the top of the water. Again, have the children describe what they see. (This experiment can be followed by the Marbleized Paper activity on page 105.)

4. Water expands when it freezes. Put water in a paper cup. Mark the water level on the outside of the cup. Put the cup in the freezer. What happens?

   If you have room in the school freezer, or if it is freezing outside, try this simple experiment: fill a plastic milk container with water. Ask students for observations about how the container looks (students can record this information by drawing the container). Cap the container and set it out to freeze. Ask for observations again. How did the container change?

5. Water is clear. When it looks darker, it is because of the dirt in it (for example, pond water looks brown). This can be demonstrated by straining pond or puddle water through cheese cloth or coffee filters. As the dirt is removed from the water, the water gets lighter. Water also appears to take on the color of its container. Pour water from a clear container to a colored container (such as a plastic cup). Swimming pools are often painted blue or have a blue liner inside. The pool water, although clear, then looks blue.

6. Over three fourths of the earth is covered with water. Our bodies are predominantly water. Water is a part of many things we might not realize at first sight. Illustrate this by having the children bring in juice labels. Help them check the list of ingredients for water. Keep in mind that manufacturers are required to list ingredients in order of their predominance.

7. Water is heavy. One gallon weighs over eight pounds. This becomes an economic factor for companies that produce products made with water. Bring to class a package of sweetened drink mix, a can of frozen concentrate, and a can of ready-to-serve juice. Have the class compare the prices of the three products. Ask them also to comment on packaging and storing requirements (frozen products usually need more sophisticated packaging than dry ones).

8. People called "dowsers" use forked hazel sticks, or "divining rods" to locate water. They walk with the rods extended until they feel a tug, which tells them that water is below.

Water Facts (continued)

Potable (drinkable) water exists in the ground almost everywhere on the earth. The depth to which one must dig to find it varies with the kind of soil on top, recent weather conditions, and the level of the water table (see page 97).

9. A well is a hole in the ground dug deeply enough so that it reaches below the water table. If Jack and Jill were getting their water from a well on a hill, the well would have looked something like this:

10. Water exists in three forms or states: liquid (water), solid (ice), and gas (vapor). Water freezes at 32° F (0° C) and boils, giving off vapor, at 212° F (100° C).

11. Why did Jack and Jill need a bucket of water? Have the class brainstorm different uses of water. Or give each student or pair of students a piece of paper. Have them fold the paper into four boxes. In each box, ask the children to write and illustrate a different use for water (for example, washing a car, getting a drink, and taking a bath). Ask children to share their ideas, and write them on the board. How many different uses for water can the class think of?

12. Ask the students to recount times when they have been injured or ill. What made them feel better: being taken care of by a parent, visits from friends, get-well cards?

    Reproduce the Get-Well Card on page 118 and have it available at a learning center for students to use when a classmate is sick.

    As a homework or seatwork assignment have the children draw get-well presents on the Three Gifts for Jack and Jill blackline master, page 119.

Water Conservation Ideas

The following is a list of things children can do to help conserve water. This list can be discussed at school, then shared with family members at home.

1. Run water only when you are using it. Don't let it run while you are doing something else, such as brushing your teeth or scrubbing the dishes. A running faucet can let more than 3 gallons of water a minute go down the drain.

2. Your toilet uses 5 to 7 gallons of water each time it is flushed. Displace water in your toilet tank with a plastic liter soda or juice bottle filled with water. Water conservation kits may also be purchased at the hardware store. These kits contain a plastic bag to fill with water, along with the hardware necessary to hang it inside the tank. These displacement devices save water while keeping the pressure high enough to flush the toilet. (Do not displace the water in the tank with a brick. Pieces of the brick can come off and damage the plumbing system.)

3. Use water from the wading pool to water the lawn or the garden.

4. When watering the lawn with a sprinkler, do not allow the water to fall on the sidewalks or street.

   The best time to water a lawn is in the early morning. Water evaporates during the day when the sun is at its hottest. Watering at night could cause fungus to grow on the lawn.

5. Make sure the dishwasher and washing machine are full before running them.

Nursery Rhyme Drama

Materials

■ Flannel Board Cutouts blackline master, page 111 (optional)

■ Finger Puppets blackline master, page 112 (optional)

Drama is an excellent way to experience problem solving, as well as practice language. This activity is a group effort.

Procedure

Begin to say the nursery rhyme and stop after "down":

> Jack and Jill
>
> Went up the hill
>
> To fetch a pail of water.
>
> Jack fell down...

Ask students, "How can we get Jack back up that hill so he can finally get his pail of water?" Brainstorm with the class different ways Jack can get back up the hill, and list these suggestions on the board. Divide the class into small groups of two or three. Have each group decide on a method for getting up the hill and pantomime it for the rest of the class. Then let the class guess how each group solved the problem.

Variation: Reproduce the Jack and Jill Flannel Board Cutouts and blackline masters (pages 111–112) for your students. Invite them to retell the rhyme using these figures.

Digging a Well

Materials

- aquarium (or large glass bowl)
- sand
- spoon
- water

Gravity is the force that pulls rain down through the surface of the earth until the water reaches a non-permeable layer. There it spreads out horizontally, forming what is known as a water table.

Groundwater can be found below the surface of the earth if one digs deeply enough. A well is simply a hole that dips below the level of the groundwater and allows the water to seep into that hole. In this demonstration the sand represents the loose outermost layer of the earth. The bottom of the aquarium is the nonporous earth layer which helps to form the water table. The water is precipitation which seeps into the ground.

Procedure

Put a 4-inch layer of sand in the bottom of the aquarium or bowl. Pour water into the aquarium so that it reaches a level of about 2 inches. Because of gravity, the water sinks down into the earth (sand) until it is stopped by rock or other nonporous material. As the water levels out along this layer it is forming the water table.

Dig a hole into the sand up against the glass so that it is visible to the class. The hole or "well" will fill up to the level of the aquarium's "water table."

Follow-up: Ask for observations or comments about the demonstration. Scoop out some of the water from the aquarium's well and ask where more water comes from as the well water is used (precipitation—rain or snow—and/or from the water table leveling out).

Water Music

Materials

- 8 bottles of the same size and shape (spaghetti sauce jars also work well)

- water

- funnel

- wooden spoon

Sound is perceived when vibrating air hits a person's eardrums and causes them to vibrate. In this experiment, water vibrations set air in motion. The air vibrations travel through the air to the students' ears. The different pitches heard are determined by the varying levels of water in the bottles.

Procedure

Make a musical scale using the eight bottles filled to different water levels. Using the funnel, fill the first bottle with at least 2 1/2 inches of water (any less doesn't sound much different from an empty bottle).

Into the remaining seven bottles, pour slightly more water each time so that when you tap each bottle with the wooden spoon the pitch sounds lower than the previous bottle. You will have to add or subtract water until the scale sounds just right.

Have the children take turns playing the water music. Make sure that they see how the water moves when the bottle is struck. Leave the bottles in a corner of the room so that everyone has a chance to try them.

Extension: Once you have found the proper water levels for a scale, assign letters or numbers to them so that the children can play songs. Here are two familiar tunes to play using the number values, with 1 being the fullest bottle and 8 the least filled.

Copy these songs onto 5-by-7-inch cards and place them near the bottles.

"Twinkle, Twinkle, Little Star"
1-1 5-5 6-6 5
4-4 3-3 2-2 1
5-5 4-4 3-3 2
5-5 4-4 3-3 2
1-1 5-5 6-6 5
4-4 3-3 2-2 1

"Mary Had A Little Lamb"
3 2 1 2 3 3 3
2 2 2 3 5 5
3 2 1 2 3 3 3
3 2 2 3 2 1

Observing the Water Cycle: Making Terrariums

Materials

- 2- or 3-liter plastic soda bottles (1 for each student)

- plastic wrap

- rubber bands

- soil

- seeds or small plants (Small plants can often be purchased at nurseries for a nominal price. These seem to work better than seeds because children can focus on the water cycle within their terrariums rather than the sprouting, or lack of sprouting, of the seeds.)

Few children realize that clouds are primarily made up of moisture in the air. As clouds grow heavy with moisture, precipitation occurs, bringing snow or rain to the ground. Some of the ground moisture evaporates, creating more moisture in the air (and thus creating more clouds). This process is known as the water cycle.

Creating terrariums gives children the opportunity to see the water cycle in action. Water from the soil evaporates, creating a "cloud" of water on the inside lid of the terrarium. Water from this cloud then "rains" down on the plants and soil again.

Procedure

Prepare the soda bottles by removing the labels and cutting off the top third of the bottle. This can be done by carefully poking a hole in the bottle with scissors, then cutting around. (This should be done ahead of time by an adult. If you send directions home with the request for bottles, children can bring them in already prepared.)

Put soil in the bottles. With a finger, dig a small hole and plant the seeds or plants. Generously water the soil, then cover each bottle with a piece of plastic wrap. Put one or two rubber bands around the wrap to make sure the terrarium is sealed.

Have children observe over a period of days as water collects on the plastic wrap to form a "cloud." Observations can be shared and recorded in science journals.

Food Dye Tie Dye

Materials

- white paper towels (thicker brands work better than the economy brands)

- bowls or muffin tins

- food coloring

- water

- newspaper

Here is an art project that uses the capillary action of water to make designs that look like tie-dyeing. The food dye makes the water's movement easy to track.

Procedure

Cover your work area with newspaper. Make four different colors of dye by mixing a few drops of the coloring with water in each of the bowls or muffin tins (see the back of the food coloring box for variations in color).

Have each child fold a paper towel into halves, quarters, then eighths. Tell students that the final design will reflect whether they did this symmetrically or not; they may choose.

Let each child dip a corner of the paper towel into one of the bowls of dye and watch as the dye climbs up the paper towel. This is called capillary action.

For an intricate pattern, have students dip different parts of the towel into different colors. They do not need to saturate the towel to distribute the color; the capillary action of the water alone moves the dye through the paper.

When students have finished dipping, have them unfold the paper towel and set it on newspaper to dry. Mounting it on construction paper can accentuate the design while giving the paper towel extra support. The towel can also be used as wrapping paper at holiday time.

Floating Experiment

Materials

- small buckets or plastic containers for holding water (you will need one for every two or three students)

- small plastic bags of materials for each group (the materials for each group can vary; what follows is a suggested list)

- pencils

- paper clips

- crayons

- paper

- pencil erasers

- feathers

- plastic silverware

- metal silverware

- yarn pieces

- Floats/Sinks blackline master (1 for each student), page 113

In this experiment, children predict which items will sink in water and which will float. They then test their predictions and record their results.

Procedure

Divide the class into groups of two or three. Pass out the buckets and bags of materials.

Have the group predict which of their items will float in the water and which will sink. Based on these predictions, children sort their items into a "sinks" pile and a "floats" pile.

Pass out the containers of water and have the children test their predictions by dropping their items into the water one at a time.

Pass out the Floats/Sinks sheets. Have the children draw and label items that floated or sank in the appropriate column.

Variation: This project can be set up in a learning center for students to explore on their own.

Extension: Students can take the completed worksheet home and explain the activity to their families. With help, they can add items from home to the "floats" and "sinks" lists.

Water Absorption

Materials

■ paper cups of water (1 for each group)

■ eyedroppers or straws (1 for each group)

■ 1 small plastic bag for each group containing:

■ ice cream stick

■ paper towel

■ wax paper

■ foil

■ cardboard

■ Absorbs? blackline master (1 for each student), page 114

This experiment allows children to predict, test, and record which materials absorb water and which do not.

Procedure

Draw a simple picture on the "Absorbs?" blackline master (page 114) of each item to be tested, label it, and reproduce the master for the students.

Divide the class into teams of two or three and distribute the materials.

Show the teams how to release a few drops of water from an eyedropper or straw. (Put the straw into the cup of water and put a finger over the top of the straw. Raise the straw up and out of the cup and then move the finger off, allowing a few drops of water to be released.) You may want to have the children practice this.

Explain to the children that they will be testing the materials in their bags for absorption. They are to put a few drops of water on each item. If the water soaks into it, making the material wet, then the material has absorbed the water. Students must locate the item on their worksheets and check the Yes box. If the water lies in drops on top of the material, then that material does not absorb water and students must check No on their worksheets. You may want to go over the list of materials and try one together.

Allow time for the children to experiment with the items in their bags. Encourage them to test other items for absorption and to record their results on their worksheets.

Extension: After the class has finished experimenting, hold up some items that were not tested (such as a piece of paper). Based on what they now know about absorption, have the children predict whether or not the material absorbs water. Test the predictions to see whether they are correct.

Safety Lesson:
Reading Warning Signs

Materials

- pictures of warning signs such as STOP, YIELD, or DANGER (children may be able to provide these from magazines at home)

- crayons

- paper

Safety issues are especially important for young children who may be playing outside without constant adult supervision. This lesson helps make children aware of warning signs in their environment.

Procedure

Brainstorm reasons why Jack might have fallen down the hill. Was the hill slippery? Did he trip over rocks?

Share the pictures of the warning signs with the class. Ask whether the children recognize any of the words. What do the signs mean? What kind of warning sign might have helped Jack? If possible, take a walk outside near your school and look for different kinds of warning signs. Discuss why the signs are there.

Brainstorm warning words and make a list of them. Using crayons and paper, children can make signs warning Jack and Jill of danger on the hill. Children may want to use words from the class list.

Extension: Look around the classroom or the school. Ask students whether they see a place that needs a warning sign. Help students make signs and place them in the necessary spots.

Watercolor Sequencing

Materials

- watercolor paper

- watercolor paints

- brushes

- water

"Jack and Jill" is an easy rhyme to learn, and one that children are likely to know before coming to your class. Take advantage of this familiarity by using the rhyme to introduce sequencing. If students can understand the concept at this basic level, it will be easier to understand when it is applied to more complex stories.

Procedure

Divide the class into groups of three. Have each group member illustrate a different part of the rhyme, using watercolor paints. (Jack and Jill went up the hill to fetch a pail of water./Jack fell down and broke his crown/and Jill came tumbling after.)

When the paintings are dry, ask the members of each group to arrange themselves in the right order and share their pictures. Display the paintings in groups of three with the corresponding parts of the rhyme written above them.

Marbleized Paper

Materials

- food coloring

- vegetable oil

- water

- 9-by-13-inch baking dishes (1 for each color desired)

- newspaper

- cups

- tablespoon

- white paper (1 sheet for each student; have students write their names on the back)

Water is the universal solvent—almost everything dissolves in it. Oil is one substance that will not dissolve in water. In this project, water-based food coloring trapped in beads of vegetable oil floats on the water's surface. When paper is laid on the surface, the exposed food coloring is absorbed by the paper, while that trapped in oil leaves a blank space. This gives the paper a marbleized look.

Procedure

Spread newspaper over your work area, and also over a place for drying the finished designs.

For each color of marbleized paper to be created, you will need a separate baking dish filled with water. In a cup, mix one tablespoon of vegetable oil with several drops of food coloring. Pour the oil-food coloring mixture over the water in the baking dish.

Have students lay the paper briefly on the water surface, then gently pull it off. Let them experiment with different designs by tilting the wet paper from side to side; the dye will streak across the paper while it is still wet. Lay the paper on the newspaper to dry.

Discuss the procedure with the class. Why did some spaces on the paper stay white while others absorbed the dye? Where does the oil go when it is put into the water? Does it sink, float, or mix with the water?

Extension: Use the marbleized paper for the cover of a home-made book.

Overview of Blackline Masters

Nursery Rhyme: Jack and Jill: See Day 1 of "Sharing Rhymes with the Class: A Basic Format," page x.

Cloze Activity: Partners take turns reading the rhymes, then determine which words complete the rhyme.

Word Making: -ill Words: Children cut out the letters and put them together to make words that end with ill.

Word Making: -ack Words: Children cut out the letters and put them together to make words that end with ack.

Flannel Board Cutouts: Color Jack and Jill, mount the figures on oaktag, and glue pieces of felt on the back. Students can use cutouts to act out the rhyme.

Finger Puppets: Have students color the puppets, glue them onto oaktag, and then cut them out. Students can use the puppets to act out the rhyme. (The finger holes are difficult to cut. Start the cutting for the children by making a hole with a hole punch in each circle.)

Floats/Sinks: Use with the Floating Experiment activity, page 101.

Absorbs?: Use with the Water Absorption activity, page 102.

Handwriting: Children fill in their own names in place of Jack, then trace the rhyme as a hand-writing exercise (good for seatwork or home-work).

Book to Illustrate: Reproduce pages 116 and 117 back to back. Have the students fold the pages in half, staple them into book form, and then illus-trate them. Illustrating requires that the chil-dren read and understand the text. Subsequently, their own illustrations serve as context clues when they reread the rhyme.

Get-Well Card: Reproduce this card for use in a learning center during the unit or all year around. The children can write cards to Jack and Jill or to classmates when they are sick.

Three Gifts for Jack and Jill: This activity is a good homework assignment. The students draw three items that Jack and Jill might need or want while recovering from their fall down the hill. This activity can be extended by asking children to bring in one item that they would want if they were sick or hurt.

Jack and Jill

Jack and Jill
Went up the hill
To fetch a pail of water.
Jack fell down
And broke his crown
And Jill came tumbling after.

Jack and Jill

Jack and Jill
Went up the hill
To fetch a pail of water.
Jack fell down
And broke his crown
And Jill came tumbling after.

Jack and Jill

Jack and Jill
Went up the hill
To fetch a pail of water.
Jack fell down
And broke his crown
And Jill came tumbling after.

Jack and Jill

Jack and Jill
Went up the hill
To fetch a pail of water.
Jack fell down
And broke his crown
And Jill came tumbling after.

Name_____

Partner's Name_____

> Jack and Jill
> Went up the hill
> To fetch a pail of water.
>
> Jack fell down
> And broke his crown
> And Jill came tumbling after.

Fill in the blanks:

> Jack and Jill
>
> Went up the _____
>
> To fetch a pail of water.
>
> _____ fell down
>
> And broke his _____
>
> And _____ came tumbling after.

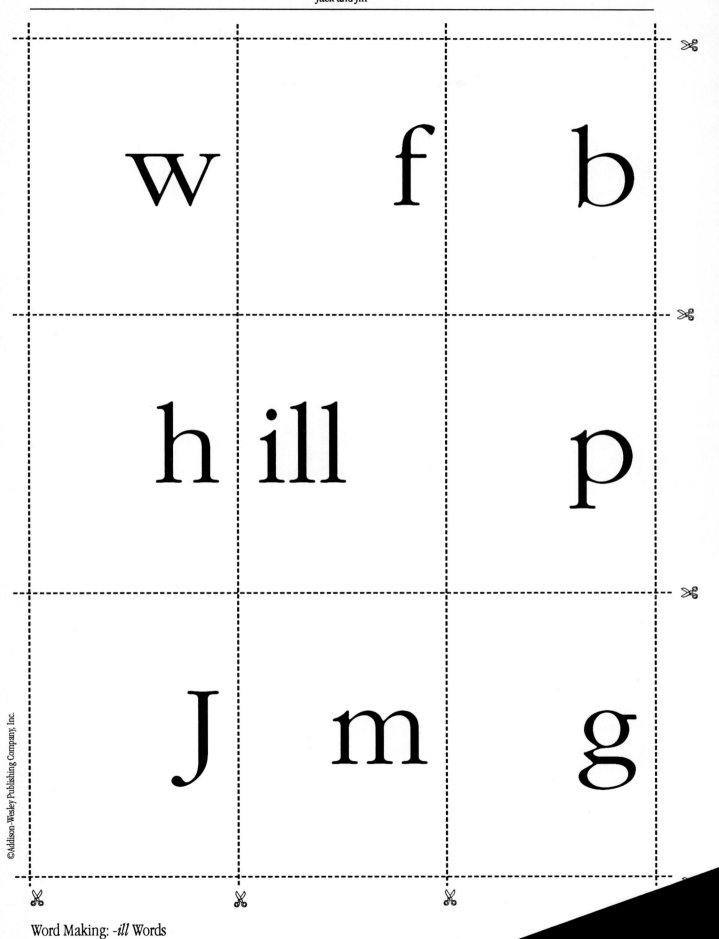

w

f

b

h ill

p

J

m

g

Word Making: *-ill* Words

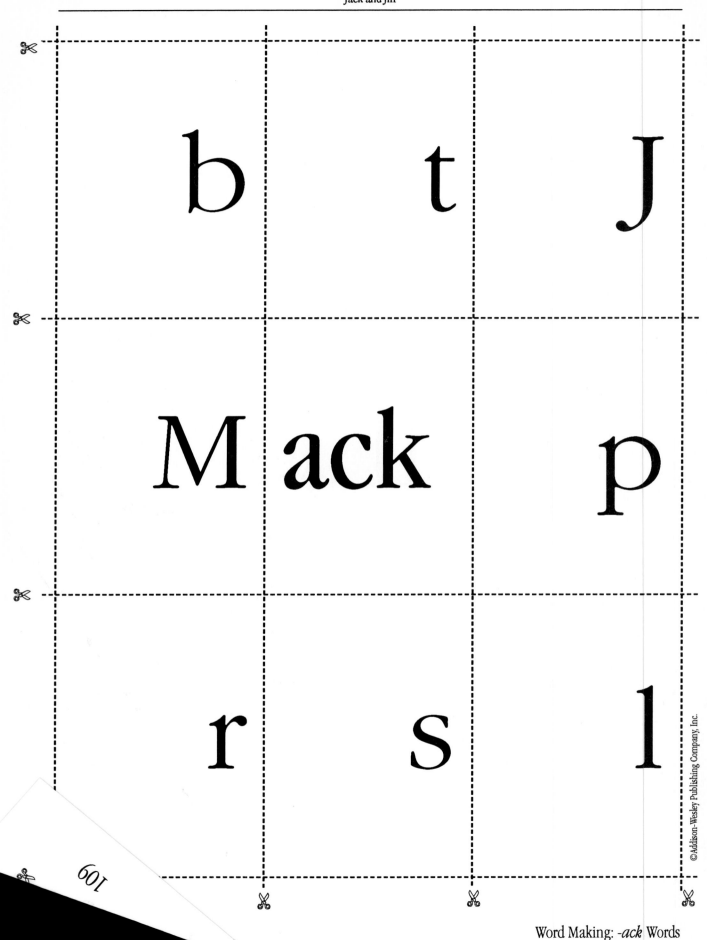

b   t   J

M ack   p

r   s   l

Word Making: *-ack* Words

Finger Puppets

FLOATS | SINKS

Absorbs?	Yes	No

Name _____ Trace the rhyme and fill in your name.

_____ and Jill

Went up the hill

To fetch a pail

of water.

_____ fell down

And broke ____ crown

And Jill came

tumbling after.

Jack and Jill

Illustrated by _____

And Jill came tumbling after.

4

Jack fell down
and broke his crown,

3

Jack and Jill went up the hill
to fetch a pail of water.

2

Get-Well Card

Name_____

Draw 3 gifts you might give to Jack and Jill after their fall.

Three Gifts for Jack and Jill

Appendix

Additional Rhyme Activities

Nursery Rhyme Mural

On several pieces of butcher paper, write rhymes that lend themselves to illustration. Small groups can collaborate to plan and then illustrate each rhyme. The rhymes can be grouped together to make a Mother Goose mural.

Mother Goose Day

On a particular day, have each child dress as a favorite nursery rhyme character. Characters can recite their poems or act them out together. Children who do not wish to dress up can create a mural, diorama, or poster depicting their rhyme.

Nursery Rhyme Stories

Help the whole class or small groups make up stories based on the nursery rhymes. Have the children imagine where the rhyme occurs and why the characters act as they do. For example, who were Jack and Jill? Why did they need water? What happened after they fell?

The stories can be made into big books and illustrated by the children.

Mystery Characters

Each week during the unit, select a "mystery character of the week." Each day, share one clue about the character's identity. For example, for "Little Miss Muffet," the clues might include an item that she would use (for example, bug spray), a brief tape recording of sounds she might make (for example, a shriek, then the sound of running footsteps), or a single word clue (for example, *arachnophobia*).

Clues should be difficult at first, then get increasingly easier as the week goes on. Children can record their guesses in a secret ballot box.

Verbal Characters

This activity enables students to recall different nursery rhymes and to infer the thoughts of their favorite characters. Before beginning this activity, display some comic strips in which the characters talk through "voice balloons." Explain the function of a voice balloon as a way of showing what the characters are saying.

Ask the students to select a favorite nursery rhyme character. Brainstorm comments each character might make (for example, Jack from "Jack and Jill" might complain that his head hurts; Peter's wife from "Peter, Peter, Pumpkin Eater" might demand freedom from her pumpkin shell by yelling, "Let me out!")

Students create their characters by first cutting the shape of a person out of construction paper (people templates for the students to trace and cut are helpful here), then adding features and clothing with yarn, material scraps, pieces of wallpaper and construction paper, buttons, and so on. When the characters are complete, have students trace and cut out a "voice balloon" and dictate to the teacher or adult helper what they want the character to say. The words can be written in pencil, then traced over in crayon or marker by the students.

Make a mural by gluing students' characters and balloons on butcher paper. Let students add the background scenery.

Nursery Rhyme Cooking

One, Two Apple Salad

This recipe is in the rhyme. To begin, each child will need a small cup or bowl, a spoon for stirring, and a plastic knife for cutting.

One, two, an apple for you
(each child is given some apple slices to chop into small pieces)
Three, four, nuts and raisins galore
(add a small handful of raisins and nuts to the chopped apple)
Five, six, celery sticks
(each child is given a celery stick to chop and add to the salad)
Seven, eight, mayo is great
(stir in a spoonful of mayonnaise)
Nine, ten, a pinch of cinnamon!
(add a pinch of cinnamon, stir, and enjoy!)

Peter, Peter, Pumpkin Bread

Preheat oven to 325° F. Grease and flour 3 large loaf pans.
Mix together the following:
3 1/2 C flour
2 t baking soda
1 1/2 t salt
1 1/2 t cinnamon
1 t nutmeg
3 C sugar
1 C raisins (optional)
To the above, add:
1 C vegetable oil
4 eggs, lightly beaten
2/3 C water
1 1/2 C canned pumpkin pie filling
Pour into pans. Bake at 325°F for approximately 1 hour.

Little Miss Muffet Spiders
1 small-size can Chinese noodles
8 oz chocolate morsels
Melt the chocolate morsels in a double boiler or in the microwave. Transfer to bowl and stir in Chinese noodles. Coat thoroughly. Drop by the teaspoonful onto waxed paper. Put into the refrigerator to chill.

Humpty Dumpty Egg Yolk Paint
refrigerated butter cookie dough
1/4 t water
3 or 4 drops food coloring
1 egg yolk
Roll out cookie dough and cut into shapes (preferably nursery rhyme shapes). Mix remaining ingredients together and paint onto cookies before baking. Bake as directed.

Other Components of the Reading/Writing Classroom

The activities described in this unit form only a small piece of the language pie. Other activities, including self-selected reading and writing activities, are critical in nurturing language growth. In a reading/writing classroom, the teacher acts as a facilitator, providing opportunities for students to read and write for a variety of meaningful purposes. Students are free to select among these activities.

Self-Selected Writing

Students need to have ample time to practice writing by writing for a variety of purposes and for a variety of audiences. Time should be set aside each day for students to write about topics of their own choosing. Young writers learn letter-sound relationships and word patterns as they write. The activities described in this unit provide opportunity for teachers to model writing for their students. As a teacher records predictions and observations on the board, she or he is modeling such aspects of writing as left-right progression, letter-sound correspondence, and formation of letters. The teacher also models how to record information and make lists. Students then need time to experiment with their own writing in a risk-free environment.

Personal journals offer a chance for students to write about self-selected topics. Topics are student-generated, and teachers respond to, rather than correct the journal entries. Beginning writers often use both pictures and letters to convey meaning. Children use invented spelling to approximate letters and words. Strings of consonant letters may initially be used; as students begin to make letter-sound connections, their approximations will begin to resemble conventional spelling.

Teachers can further model conventional writing by writing a response while the student watches, saying each word as it is written. Using some of the student's own words in the response, the teacher models conventional spelling without correcting the student's approximations. The environment is risk-free; students are encouraged to try out new patterns, and all attempts at writing are applauded.

Students may choose to write about classroom experiences, and they may incorporate some of the word patterns they have explored. However, these topics and words are not mandated.

In addition to writing in journals, students are encouraged to write in a classroom writing center. This is an area of the classroom arranged by the teacher and set aside specifically for student writing. The writing center should be stocked with paper (lined and unlined, large and small), tools for writing and illustrating (pencils, crayons, markers, and so on), as well as scissors, staplers, rulers, and tape so that students can make their own books.

Let students have time to explore on their own some of the writing extensions modeled by the teacher. For example, the teacher and a small group may collaboratively write a get-well card for Jack and Jill as described in Chapter 3. After this experience, supplies may be available in the writing center for students to write their own get-well cards. Likewise, after rewriting "One, Two, Buckle My Shoe" as a large group, individuals or small groups may write their own versions in the writing center. Again, these activities are not mandated by the teacher; students may do them if they wish, or they may choose to write on their own topic.

Science Journals

Science journals provide a place for students to respond to the science activities found in each unit. These journals (commercially-made or homemade composition books) provide a meaningful writing context for students to record their observations and predictions. The teacher may model the process first by brainstorming and recording questions or predictions with the class. Students may respond to an open-ended question posed by the teacher, or they may use pictures and words to record their own questions and observations. Actual experiments may be photocopied and placed in the journals. Students can then take their journals home to retell the experience to family members. The experiment could be repeated at home. Later, using their journals as a reference, the class can collaboratively write an account of the experiments for publication in a class book or a school newspaper.

Sharing journals is an important part of the process. Students share their observations and questions with their classmates, opening the door for making comparisons and engaging in discussions. As students share, they provide a model of response that other students may want to follow.

Self-Selected Reading

No reading program would be complete without the inclusion of self-selected reading. In each of our units, the teacher leads the reading and exploration of a particular nursery rhyme. In addition to teacher-led reading, students need time to read books of their own choosing. Children select from a variety of reading materials and interact with the print on their own level. Some may practice rereading rhymes explored earlier in the day, while others may choose

to read unrelated texts. Some children with developed voice-print match may carefully read word by word, while others may "read" the pictures. After reading, students should share what they have read, either with a partner or a group. This sharing helps to spark student interest in books that others have read. Students may also respond by writing or drawing favorite parts in their journals.

Scheduling the Day

Consistent, predictable daily schedules are essential to any classroom; children feel more in control of their learning and their day when they know what to expect. At the same time, the schedule needs to be flexible enough to meet ever-changing daily demands. We've found it helpful to schedule several blocks of time throughout the day for our activities. If one block takes longer than usual on a particular day, another block can simply be shortened to make up the difference. Time for each block varies according to the day's activities. What follows is a sample schedule that we might follow on the first day of the "Jack Be Nimble" unit:

Shared Language: This block, also known as "circle time," is the first block of the day. This period might include such routines as marking the calendar and discussing the weather. Children are seated comfortably on a rug on the floor. If students had free time when they entered the classroom, take a few minutes to let them share their activities with the class. Then have students "warm up" by singing a song, performing a familiar fingerplay or movement activity, and/or choral reading a book that has been previously read and discussed.

Following the procedure described earlier in this book, introduce the rhyme "Jack Be Nimble." After completing echo and choral reading, have students predict reasons for Jack jumping over the candle and record their responses on chart paper. Then share the history of the rhyme (see Chapter 1, "Candle Facts and Ideas For Discussion").

After exploring the rhyme, let students glue the rhyme into their poetry books and return to their seats to practice reading the rhyme to a partner.

Personal Reading: Following the reading of the nursery rhyme text, give students an opportunity to read texts of their own choosing. Students may respond to the texts by telling about them to the group, or writing and drawing about them in their journals.

Personal Writing: Students have an opportunity to write on self-selected topics.

Math: Sorting, Classifying, and Patterning— Children complete the Candle Sort activity as described in Chapter 1. They explain their sorting system to other groups, then make and record a pattern with their candles.

Science: Children participate in the Candle Experiment (page 9) described in Chapter 1. Predictions are recorded on the board; responses are made in science journals and shared.

Sample Daily Schedule

8:45–9:00	Students arrive and take part in early-bird activities (self-selected or teacher-selected)
9:00–9:45	Shared language
9:45–10:15	Self-selected reading and sharing
10:15–10:30	Recess or movement activity
10:30–11:00	Self-selected writing and sharing
11:00–11:45	Specials (library, gym, music, and so on)
11:45–12:30	Math
12:30–1:15	Lunch/recess
1:15–1:30	Teacher read-aloud time
1:30–2:15	Science/social studies
2:15–3:00	Centers—children rotate through math, science, language, art, listening, and dramatic play centers. The teacher may choose to rotate groups through two or three centers at timed intervals, or allow children to self-select centers.
3:00-3:15	Students complete the day by reviewing the events and perhaps sharing center activities.

Evaluation and Record Keeping

Teachers who make the transition to a whole-language classroom usually have two concerns about evaluation: how to keep records of their students' progress, and how to condense those records into the traditional letter grades. We advocate extending whole language to the assessment process by using anecdotal, or observational records.

Anecdotal Records

We use anecdotal records to track our students' progress. These take the form of short written observations, usually made during the students' independent work time—as they write in their journals or work in learning centers. Carry a clipboard of gummed labels as you circulate among your students. Anecdotal notes focus on the achievements of the children. For example:

> E.C.N.—Using beginning consonants accurately in journal. 4-25-94
>
> Helped P.K. sound out words. 10-6-93

For speed, use children's initials. Date each entry.

Anecdotal records require practice on the part of the teacher. Admittedly, it takes more time to write your observations than to check off a skill from a provided checklist, but the value of an observational record lies in its precise description of the work of a particular student in your particular program.

Anecdotal records also provide a view of a student over time (unlike tests, which record performance only on one particular day) and thus present a truer picture of a student's progress than a check or a letter grade.

If you must use a fill-in-the-blank report card, include your comments as well. The many achievements realized in a whole-language classroom cannot be communicated with a single letter or check.

Tracking Records

At the start of the school year, make a folder for each student. These folders will be used to collect writing samples throughout the year. Keep a rubber date stamp ready to facilitate dating these samples. To help with the increased workload, recruit a fifth- or sixth-grade student to be your after-school classroom aide. She or he can help with filing and similar jobs.

Every few days transfer the gummed labels with your observations to the inside of the appropriate file folders. At conference time you will be able to present a full picture of each child's achievements to his or her parents.

Conference Binder

In addition to the writing sample folder with its gummed label anecdotal records, keep a record of your one-on-one meetings with students. Even though informal observations take place daily, make it a point to sit and talk with each student about his or her activities each week. Allow students to schedule additional conferences by putting their names on a designated spot on the board. These conferences should last about five minutes, during which the two of you discuss the student's current reading or writing project. Keep a binder with a page for each child.

For example: Name: Peter

DATE	PROJECT	OBSERVATION
10-4-92	solo reading	Uses picture clues.
	Brown Bear	Reads with rhythm.

This form will quickly let you know what a student is working on.

Checklists

Although we do not advocate using checklists as the sole form of evaluation, especially when they are imposed from outside the classroom, teacher-generated checklists can help give a quick overview of who has done what in a given time period. If you have three centers, a writing project, and a reading corner, put these activities and the weekly tasks on a checklist to be sure everyone gets to everything. The following is a sample checklist:

Week of: 9-13-93

Names	Center 1	Center 2	Center 3	Writing	Reading	Journal
Deirdre	✔				✔	
Anthony		✔	✔	✔		
Nikki	✔	✔				

One look at your list will let you see which students may need extra support in which areas. Encourage the students to "check out" with you when they've completed each task.

On a second checklist you can frame goals for your students and check them off by dating them as you first observe them. For example:

Names	Uses Invented Spelling	Uses Beginning Spelling	Uses Ending Sound	Beginning to Discover Sense of Story
Deirdre	10/22	10/15	10/15	
Anthony	9/14	9/14		
Nikki	10/22			

The Home/School Connection

Parents are often eager to share and participate in their child's learning, and should be included in the learning process. Parents can be a vital part of the classroom, contributing both time and resources. Involved and informed parents are able to reinforce and enhance skills learned in the classroom. The letters to parents on page 130 introduce them to the nursery rhyme unit and invite them to contribute necessary materials.

Dear Parents,

During the next several weeks, our class will be studying four popular Mother Goose nursery rhymes: "Jack Be Nimble"; "Star Light, Star Bright"; "Jack and Jill"; and "One, Two, Buckle My Shoe." I will be teaching with Addison-Wesley's *Star Light, Star Bright,* a teacher resource book incorporating many whole-language practices. During this unit my aim is to share the joy of language with my students.

At home, you can support this nursery rhyme unit by listening to your child read from his or her rhyme book and by discussing the related activities we will be doing. This is also the perfect time for you and your child to explore other nursery rhymes that you have at home or that you might find at your local library. Please feel free to share your favorite rhymes with us.

In addition to the rhymes, this unit includes cross-curricular hands-on activities based on the rhyme themes: candles and fire ("Jack Be Nimble"); astronomy and space travel ("Star Light, Star Bright"); counting ("One, Two, Buckle My Shoe"); and water ("Jack and Jill").

I am excited about the study we are getting ready to undertake. As the unit progresses, I would be interested in your comments and observations of what your child enjoys.

I appreciate your involvement!

Sincerely,

Dear Parents,

Will you help us collect some items to use during the Nursery Rhyme unit? We need:

　　candles (new or used, any size or shape)
　　2- or 3-liter plastic soda bottles
　　paper towel rolls
　　egg cartons
　　heavy wire coat hangers

Thanks in advance for your help.

Sincerely,